In My Mother's House

In My Mother's House

Blaque Diamond

Library of Congress Control Number:		2010903664
ISBN:	Hardcover	978-1-4500-6318-0
	Softcover	978-1-4500-6317-3
	Ebook	978-1-4500-6319-7

This book was printed in the United States of America.

To order additional copies of this book, contact:
Xlibris Corporation
1-888-795-4274
www.Xlibris.com
Orders@Xlibris.com
75784

CONTENTS

I thank God for allowing me to live long enough to see my children grow.

There is an experience that you undergo only once in a lifetime, and that experience was having my firstborn, thank you,

God

for allowing me the experience of having

Truth.

Getting a gift from God and having a dream come true is only given to a lucky few. I thank you, Lord, for my special gift,

Justice.

The third time is always the charm. You are my rabbit's foot, my four-leaf clover, you are my everything
Thank you, Jesus, for what I had hoped for,

Wise.

Thank you God for allowing me to have two special deliveries without going through the labor pains.

Iyleah and Heaven

Always love,

Ma

Note to the Reader

This is a piece of work. Some of the characters' names in this story have been changed to protect those who believe they are innocent and those who are truly innocent. Any similarities between places and situations presented in this book will make you feel as though you either lived there or visited.

And Nothing but the Truth

April 19

It was too early in the morning. Did I have a hangover or what? No, it couldn't be that. I don't drink. Okay, maybe someone drugged me. No, that's not it either. I don't do drugs, and none of my associates do drugs—at least none that I know of—and I try to be careful about being in the wrong place at the wrong time. I must be seeing things, that tube on top of my TV is blue, as in blue for boy and pink for girl. Oh God! I'm pregnant. First person I have to tell is my best friend—no, not him, but my mother.

Can you imagine having the best of both worlds; two best friends for the price of one? I mean, my mother is my ma, and she's can be my grandma too. "Ma, are you awake? I need to talk to you." I continued to knock on her bedroom door and ask if she's awake. I got right to the point. "I took a home pregnancy test, and it shows blue. Ma, I think I'm pregnant."

I thought my mother was sitting up in her bed to say she was happy for me, but the first words out of my mother's mouth was "I knew something like this was going to happen." Get real, I mean what did my mother think? I was having sex without protection, and I'm not too proud to say, in my mother's house. After all, we were sleeping in the room next to hers. Well, maybe not always sleeping, but we were in that room, my own bedroom. Finally, my very own bedroom. Anyway, I was over twenty-one and already had custody of Coffee's daughter, Melo's six-year-old son, and Tango's four-year-old son. I would make a good mother. So what was all of this for?

Maybe I'm not pregnant. You know how some test are, they're not always 100 percent accurate and barely 50 percent spill proof. I'll go to the doctor on Monday and find out for sure. Once they draw my blood and get urine, I'll know then if I am pregnant or not. Wait, was I saying this for the sake of my mother, or did I need to know for me? Look, I can't please everyone. It's not like I had big plans for myself, I only wanted to go to Howard University and study law. Besides, I'm committed to raising my niece and nephews, and I didn't want to be another person in their life who walked away from them.

Okay, back to the situation at hand. I should get the results back in two days, so for the next two days, I kept myself busy. I had an appointment with the welfare worker, she said she needed to see my enrollment forms for the Mayer School of Fashion. Can you believe it my worker was trying to close my case. I was told that fashion design school was not a real school and that it was not on the work activity list for families receiving public assistance. I was told I would need to either enroll in an approved program set by the state or get a job. Well, that is easier said than done. Not everyone was hiring, and those who were hiring only wanted certain kinds of people, and those people were bright, light, or damn near white.

April 23

We were on Jamaica Avenue, and Tango was with me. As we got closer to the doctor's office, I thought to myself I better think fast because I didn't want Tango to know. So I said, "Hey, Tango, Mommy may want something from the pizza parlor, and I have to run upstairs to get something. Can you call her and tell her where we are and ask her what would she like to eat? And we will bring it in we get back around the way." Around the way was not too far from the boulevard. You know, where the red, black, and green rock is on Farmers Boulevard and Liberty Avenue.

"Excuse me, miss. I was here on Monday and took a blood test. Could you let me know what the results are? And can you do me a favor? My brother is with me, and I don't want him to know, so if you see this guy who is six feet four and looks like Samuel L. Jackson coming up the steps, would you jot the results down on a piece of paper? Thanks."

Sh——, here he comes, and she didn't come back with the results yet.

Positive

"All right, Tango, we can go now. Did Mommy say what she wanted?" Oh boy, that's not what I wanted to say, but that's the first thing I could think of without him knowing. Okay, what was the big secret? He would find out anyway, that's if he sticks around long enough. You see, Tango is a playa, playa, but in a good kinda way. You know what I mean. He is the type of brother that every sister would want and every other woman wanted.

"Tango, I'll call Ma and see if she wants anything else. Ma, I got the results back, and I'm pregnant. Ma, don't tell anyone, especially if he calls. Just say you don't know where I went. Tango, can you take this home to Ma? I have to make another stop for Mommy, she wants me to get her some fish from the market. Thanks."

Now I know that was a lie, but there were a few things I wanted to get, and I wanted to get them by myself. *Undershirts, Socks, Bibs, and Washcloths.* They are all so cute. And they must be in white since it is too early to tell whether I'm having a boy or a girl. Should I take the bus, or should I stop at the bus terminal on 165th Street and take a cab? Because the bus ride may shake up the baby. Wait a minute, I'm tripping. The bus ride is not going to shake up the baby, but it would be nice to see if someone will get up and give a pregnant woman a seat. Okay, I'm tripping again.

Oh boy, there she is—my sister Coffee, sitting in the window with that stupid grin on her face. And all I could think of was the *Titanic* you know; loose lips sinks ships. Mommy must have told her. And after I asked her not to. But that's all right, the bags I was carrying would have given it away. One was from Cookies, and the other one was from Young World. "Okay here we go. It's official. I'm pregnant, damn can she do anything else but grin?" You would think she was the one that was pregnant. God, I hope not. I honestly think she would be too old to have another baby. Besides I'm already taking care of her daughter.

I hid all the baby things and bags in the closet because I didn't want him to see them just in case he stopped by my house. I didn't want him to see me this way. I was crying for about an hour, not because I was pregnant, but because I just realized it took me so many years to lose this weight, and I finally looked good. I was beginning to feel good in my own skin. I mean from a size 22 pants to a size 13 pants and from a size 10 sneakers to size 5 sneakers. Now this was the look I've been trying for all my life, and being pregnant was just going to make me fat again. I spent most of the day upstairs in my room, wondering, *How am I going to care for four children all by myself?* I started to laugh. Who would have ever thought that the big fat homely looking black girl from up the street was having a baby? Thank you, God!

You know, I used to resent having the bedroom next to the bathroom, but not now. I figure when I get morning sickness I could make it to the toilet. As a matter of fact, I'm feeling a little sick now. Maybe it's all the excitement of the pregnancy. I'll lie down for a little while, and maybe I will feel better later.

Later that day, Phar and his wife, Popcorn, called me from the boulevard to see if I wanted to go with them to the movies. I told them I wasn't feeling well, but Popcorn said he was with them. I told her no again and that I was going to stay home, so I hung up the phone. The phone rang again, and it was him. He asked me to meet them on the boulevard and go to the movies with them and that he had something to talk to me about. He said that a friend of ours told him that we should talk. This lady could not hold water even if Jack and Jill were helping her carry the bucket, but I knew she meant well. I met them at Farmers Boulevard, and we took a cab to Queens Village Movies, where we ordered two pizza pies. No, they both weren't for me. Besides, Popcorn was pregnant too, and he and Phar were also big eaters. I mean, you should see the size of these guys. Both of them had to be at least six feet and some change and weighed about 270 pounds apiece.

I think he knows that I'm pregnant. My mother must have placed a loudspeaker here at the cabstand and announced it to everyone because by the time I reached the boulevard, everyone I knew was hugging me and saying congratulations. I guess we will sit up most of the night talking. I knew Popcorn knew because she was grinning from the time we got in the cab up until we ordered the pizza. Come to find out we were due around the same time. We talked and laughed throughout the entire movie. It was funny though, everyone thought we were sisters. They would ask us who was older. They even thought we were lying when we told them that we were not sisters, but we were very close friends. To tell you the truth, I am glad I had someone to go through this pregnancy with, that's if I make it through the pregnancy. I started feeling a little sick. As a matter of fact, I started to feel a lot of pain in my lower right side. I knew it was not my appendix, I had it taken out when I was ten years old.

That night, he stayed over, and I was happy. He held me all night, but I was still in pain. So the next morning, I went to the hospital without telling him. I waited until he left. I arrived at the emergency room of Mary Immaculate Hospital, where the doctor told me that I would need to get undressed so I could be examined. So I got undressed and waited for him to check my heartbeat, but instead he pulled these things out from under the table. I asked him what were those for. He told me that I needed to place my feet in it and spread my legs as wide as I could. He must be crazy, I wasn't letting him go there. Besides,

I never had one of those exams before. I didn't need to. They brought in a female doctor, and she examined me, but to be safe they were admitting me into the hospital.

My dad came to visit me in the hospital when they were just about to take me down for a sonogram. They thought I was having an ectopic pregnancy (miscarriage). My dad didn't know why I was in the hospital. He just thought I was sick, but when he found out that I was pregnant, he told me not to come to his job and for me, not to call him, he told me that he had nothing to say to me anymore. And all this from a man who only had to pay $20 a week per child for child support. I guess he thought that was too much because he had seven children, which was costing him $560 a month, not including the $20 a week alimony to my mother—giving him a grand total of $640 in support to a family he helped create.

He should have been happy by now. I mean, I was the youngest, and his big cash problems were over—no more child-support payments. All his children were over eighteen years of age anyway, there was this rumor about my father having a child by this German woman, but who cared? The man left when I was six years old. At least that's what I was told. I don't even remember him living in the house. My brothers and sisters had stories and memories that they laughed about but me I had nothing.

I often thought he had a lot of nerve. I was seventeen years old when I started raising my niece, the daughter of Coffee (his oldest child), and I later gained custody of his two grandsons by his sons (my brothers). I graduated from high school, never had a problem with the law, didn't do drugs, and was in by 10:00 p.m., and even as an adult, I told my mother where I was and when I was coming and going. He acted as if he was sending me to an Ivy League school with an allowance. I thought, for once he would be happy for me, but he just left the hospital, and I was glad. That was one more thing I didn't have to stress about. Good news came anyway, the doctors told me I could go home. I was told to stay off my feet for the next couple of weeks and try to relax.

Boy, they couldn't wait until I went into the hospital before they removed the piano from the house. I told my mom and her sister that I wanted to keep the piano. I thought if I had a little girl, I could give her piano lessons. Besides, the piano looked so good where it was. What else would fill the living room of an eleven-bedroom home? You should have seen it—this place was my palace. It was everything to me, it made me feel safe even when I wasn't. It was a place that had its own place for me to be me. You see, the walls were my conversation piece. It would listen to all my secrets, the steps would cradle me when I needed to cry, and the bathroom is where I found peace of mind, but my favorite place was my stoop. Some people may call it the front porch, but this is a place where I was able to dream, I mean really dream, of all the possibilities inside of me, but who was I fooling? Where was I ever going to go, and who would ever want to be with me or ever be my friend? I wasn't the pretty sister, the nice-looking daughter, the fun-to-be-around aunt, or the cousin anyone wanted to know. I . . . just . . . existed.

You know, there were times when I didn't think this guy loved me, but who cared? I was going to have a baby. I stopped going to fashion school and stayed home and watched other girls from the neighborhood have their babies. One girl had her baby in July, one in August, and one even in October—all boys. I knew when it was my turn that I would have a girl. "What are you waiting for? Are you coming out?" I asked her as if she could answer. But if the *we* now could talk to the *us* then, I'll bet you would have never wanted to come out, especially after all that has happened.

I received a phone call from this girl, and she described everything that I was wearing, and she also told me that I was fooling around with her husband. She said that nobody was going to have a baby by her husband but her. This simple-minded chick invited me to meet her on Farmers Boulevard. She was going to kick my a—, and if I didn't meet her, she was going to take my baby from the hospital the minute the baby was born. I called downstairs to my girl, Freeport, and made a few more phone calls. And within minutes, we were on Farmers Boulevard, but I didn't see her. I knew I didn't know her, but I would have recognized her in a split second because I knew everyone from up there. She would have presented herself as being someone new to the neighborhood, and that would have been all she wrote. Don't get me wrong, I don't and won't ever fight over any man, but when you threaten to take my baby from me, you either are in a rush to die, or you must have dialed the wrong number.

She called me back when I got home and told me she just saw me go into the house. Not only did she have my phone number, but she knew where I lived, and she also told me that she got my phone number out of his pants pocket last night when his as_ was supposed to have been down south, burying his sister, the liar. My niece told me that she just spotted him at the Encore on Jamaica Avenue, but you know, she could have him because he is not worth it or worth my baby's life. So I took precautions during my next clinic appointment. My doctor said that my pressure was up and he wanted to know if everything was okay. I had already gained fifty pounds, and he was worried, so I told him what I was going through and I also mentioned the threat against my baby. So he called the hospital administrators.

I spoke to the social worker, and they red-flagged my file so that when I was admitted into the hospital, a security guard and police officer would guard the delivery room. Once I delivered the baby, the security guard would guard me around-the-clock while the police officer would guard the baby, but just until we were discharged from the hospital. I went to the district attorney's office with my complaint, and they issued me an order of protection, as well as papers to serve her to appear in court. She had to answer to the threat she made. The first time we went to court, she showed up and came up with some story that had the case postponed, but on our second appearance, she did not show up, and the judge ordered a warrant for her arrest. Besides that, her lawyer entered into court a judgment against her for a bounced check. She knew she had to get out of dodge, so she headed for Virginia. But if I wanted her, I knew where I could get her. But as long as she kept her distance or stayed away until I delivered my baby, she would be safe. After that, who knows what may happen.

As for him, I called his house to give him a piece of my mind, but his mother answered the phone and decided she would be the bearer of news. She told me that he was married and asked me if I noticed the wedding ring that he was wearing. Only he was not wearing a wedding ring, and there was no trace of one ever being placed on that finger. I thought she was either lying, or he wasn't married long enough to have had a ring mark on it. In either case, he probably removed it whenever he was out whoring in the streets. Of course mothers are always right. The son of a gun was married—not once, but twice—and that nut case was number two.

His mother mentioned he did have a sister, (Duh). She asked me not to call her house anymore so I didn't. At this point, I should have let my oldest brother's Smith & Wesson handle him. Why did I get involved with him in the first place? I guess I made my bed and had sex in it. You know, just a year and a half before I met him, at least officially met him, I was standing in the store, talking to this lady who worked at what was known as the Spot. I had just come from school, and I was looking good, at least to my taste. I was wearing spike heels, a satin print wraparound, ankle-length skirt, and a soft blouse. I had blue contacts in my eyes, and here comes this man about six foot three or four and about 250 pounds. This was someone I thought I wanted to know.

He said hello to the lady behind the register and purchased some beer. I thought, *Well, she knows him, so I'll ask her who he is when he leaves the store.* I thought he had gone when I saw him get into this blue BMW, so I asked her what was his name? As she started to tell me his name, I noticed he was standing behind me again. I was so embarrassed, I left the store and headed home. To this day, I wondered if he heard me ask about him.

The following year, I was in a car accident and was in a lot of pain from the accident. I was supposed to go out with my girls, but I decided to fix myself some soup and get me a sandwich from Slim's. He made the best ham and cheese sandwiches on white bread. My girls lived around the corner from the store, so I decided to walk to their house and tell them that I was not going with them tonight and that they should go without me.

While walking past PS 118, this car heading in the direction of Hollis Avenue tooted its horn. I recognized the car, at least I thought I did, so I waved and said hello. The driver of the car then backed up and rolled his window down. He said, "What's up?" and I replied by saying nothing except, "How's it going with you? And have you heard from your brother?" While walking to the driver's side of the car, I thought, *This evening will not be a total loss.* You see, there was this guy from way back that enlisted in the army, and I used to write letters to him. But I never mailed them. I thought his brother would be able to tell me how he was doing. As we continued to talk, he decided to get out of the car, and the first thing in my mind was, *Oh god!* My eyes got big, and my heart was racing. This was not who I thought it was. I didn't know him from a can of paint, so I said to him, "It's been nice talking to you, and I'll see you later."

As I started to walk away, I noticed these girls from the neighborhood standing in the street, so I decided to yell over to them and say hello. They waved back and said hello. I figured, if he knew someone saw me, then he would not try anything. But he did. He grabbed me and started kissing me. I wanted to slap his face, but for some reason, I didn't. He told me to get in the car and that he would take me wherever I wanted to go. I figured, this was my chance to get away, but instead of my feet making a right my lips turned left at the end of the car, and I got in. Yes, I know, so you don't have to tell me. My mother already did. *You Don't Get into Cars with Strangers.* My lips came back to normal, and my brain did too. I told him I was getting something from the store around the corner, so he could let me out right here. I thought when I went into the store I would tell Slim's son that there was this guy that I met about five minutes ago and I got in his car. I know already; you could yell at me later, but right now I need your help so are you going to help me or what? Ok when I leave the store, I want you to get his license plate number. And if he didn't see me tomorrow by noon, he needed to give this information to the police and my family. Speaking of family, my niece lived across the street above the barbershop. I figured she was home, so I knocked on her door, but there was no answer. So I started to bang on the door, but there was still no answer, and this guy was still sitting in the car, waiting for me.

I got back in the car, and we drove off. I told him to make a left at the light, follow the traffic around until he saw another traffic light, go straight through the light and up one block, make a right turn and take this street all the way to the corner and then make a left turn. It was the big house on the right-hand side of the street. At that time, he told me that he used to know the people that lived in that house. "Oh yeah, who is this guy fooling, my family lived in this house all my life, and the people before us were Italians, so he must be lying." Then he told me the name of the people he knew—a guy named Phar and a girl named Coffee. He said he went to school with them. I then told him that they were my brother and sister.

I felt a little better, but I still didn't recognize him. He asked me if I was the only person in my family with hazel eyes. He didn't know they were contact lens, and besides I only wore the best. Anyway, I didn't know where this was going to go, so I didn't need to tell him everything about me. I just said, "Right here," and I got out of the car. We walked up the steps of my stoop, and he kissed my mother on the cheek. I thought, *Wow, my mother knows him.* But I still didn't recognize him. My niece, Sugar, the daughter of my oldest sister, Beauty, was also on the stoop. We were very close. She had just had a baby girl, I called her Porcelain, because she looked like a fine piece of china, a real doll. My niece and I had this little code that if either one of us was with a guy, we would check out his face, shoes, and clothes, and if he looked good, had nice clothes, and didn't have messed-up shoes, he gets a thumbs-up.

I ran inside and up the steps. Boy, I was taking those steps by twos. I guess the pain was gone. First I had to wake up my sister, Coffee. "Coffee, wake up. Come downstairs. I want you to see someone." I wanted to know if she knew him, so I told her his name and described him to her. She said she would need to see him first, so she did, and she knew him. I asked her if she used to date him because if she did, he would have to go. I'm not into dating someone that dated my relatives or even dated someone I knew. She said she knew him, but they didn't date. So I told her she could have my sandwich, and I went upstairs to get out of my pink-and-gray sweat suit and gray sneakers, and I put on a sweater, a miniskirt, and my moccasin boots. It was September, and I was wearing that outfit.

I felt so much better that my mother knew him, and my sister said that they all went to the same school. But he lived down the other end of Farmers Boulevard. I told my mother that I would be back later. My niece and nephews were fed and asleep, so we walked to the car. And to my surprise, he opened the car door for me and we drove off. But before we left the block, he stopped the car in front of this house and went inside. I knew the people who lived there, but I didn't know that he knew them. As a matter of fact, I wasn't speaking to them. Our families had just gotten into a fight a few days ago, so I stayed in the car.

We drove up Farmers Boulevard and turned onto Baisley Boulevard and drove until we hit Merrick Boulevard. We entered Roy Wilkins Park, where he said he had to pick up a friend after work. The park was pitch-black, and you could barely see the whites of our eyes. As he leaned over, this car pulled up behind us, and I thought, *Okay, now I'm going to be gang-raped. Well, they may get theirs off, but one of these guys won't be able to have kids when it's over. Okay, stop tripping.* It was only a police car, and the officer told us we could not park there because it was private property. I was so pissed off that I told him to drop me off at my cousin's house down the block from Wilkins Park, but wouldn't you know it, no one was home. And these are people who are up late watching TV or out front chilling. All right, now what? *Do I get back into the car or do I start walking?* It really wasn't that far, just a little over three miles.

Now where is he taking me? I guess I'm getting just what I deserved. I should have gotten out of the car when I had the chance and kept my a—at home. Okay, we were back on Farmers Boulevard, but we were going in the other direction. All right, I have an aunt that lives in that direction, and I knew she was home. She was usually in bed by 7:00 p.m. and at church every Sunday without missing a hymn. No, we didn't go that far, instead he was stopping at this store on this dark corner that was full of guys. *What is he doing?* I was hoping that he would not stop to talk to them. I wanted him to just get what he needed from the store and then get us out of there. *Now what? Did he forget his money? No, he's coming to the passenger side of the car, but why is he opening the door?* I told him I didn't feel like getting out of the car now, but he said he just wanted me to meet his friends. Okay, I had enough. I got back in the car and was ready to go home. I didn't care if my niece gave him a thumbs-up. I just wanted to go home, and I also wanted to know why he wanted me to get out of the car. He said he wanted his friends to see what I looked like, but I wanted to go *now*, so he drove me down Dunkirk and pointed out where LL Cool J's grandmother lived. So what? I already knew where she lived. He acted like he was a personal friend of their family or something. We cut down this block, and he started peeping around the corner. At first I thought he was looking to see if any cars were coming, but he had the same look in his eyes that my brothers had when they were up to no good.

As we approached my house, he asked me, What would my mother say if he didn't bring me home tonight? I told him my mother would not have anything to say. For one, I was over eighteen, and for two, he was taking me home. He opened the door, I got out of the car and I didn't say anything to him as he called my name, so he drove off. Home at last. I thought, *Just wait until I see Sugar. Thumbs-up she gave. Okay, now I have something to give her.*

A couple of days later, he called me and asked me if it was okay if he could come by for a visit. I asked him what for. I thought that night was the last time I would see him. But he came by, and we walked to the park. "Peter's Field doesn't look like it used to," he said, and I thought to myself, *Who is this guy really? Is he worth getting to know?* So we talked for a while, and he apologized for the other night. I guess he could see that I was pissed off. We were able to talk about the other night and decided to see each other again, at least whenever time allowed. He worked for some flower company, making deliveries in Manhattan, and I was still in school.

One day, he decided to surprise me by coming to my school, but I wasn't there. I had just stepped out to have lunch when a guy at McDonald's walked up to me and started talking to me. He said he noticed me entering McDonald's while he was parking his car. He asked me if he could talk to me, and I told him I was on a lunch break, so he walked me back to the school. He asked for my phone number, but I had to decline. When I got back from lunch, the secretary told me that a gentlemen was there looking for me, and he had just got on the elevator. I caught the next elevator down and saw that it was him, he was talking to the doorman who told him that I had just gone upstairs. I don't know, but it was something in his eyes. Did he just see me talking to this other guy, or was he tired from making deliveries? I asked him what he was doing here. He said that he needed to talk to me and that he wanted to take me out to lunch, only I had just come from lunch. So he said that he would meet me around the way tonight after he finished his deliveries. I told him okay.

I thought to myself, *Boy that was close.* But then I said, *I'm not married to him.* We had only been seeing each other for six months—okay, it was more than that. We had just become intimate, but I didn't belong to him, and I was my own free agent. I met him at my niece's house on Farmers Boulevard. We talked about getting our own place and only seeing one another. I told him that we couldn't just see one another. He asked why. I told him that I had other things going on. He wanted to know what they were. I just said, "Other things." He then asked me to move with him to South Carolina. I told him that I was unable to do that right now.

He then held me in his arms, and he asked me to marry him. I was shocked, I could not believe what I was hearing. I'd only been with this guy for six months, and he wanted to make it permanent. I told him that I had to tell him something, so instead of going to the movies, he walked me home. That's when I told him that I had three children. He looked shocked but was relieved when I told him they were my niece and nephews and I had custody of them. To my surprise, he said that was okay, he had already met them and knew they were good kids. He wanted them to come with us. Okay, what was going on here, and where were the cameras? For real, who put him up to this? No one did. He was serious, and I could not give him an answer tonight.

As he walked me home, he continued to make his case as I continued to tell him that I needed to think about it. I went upstairs and woke up my mother. I told her the news, and she asked me what I was going to do or rather what I was going to say. I told her that I was going to say yes, and just then, Beauty came into the bedroom and said that if I married him, she and her children would not come to the wedding. I was hurt at first because I wanted her to be right by my side, enjoying the biggest day of my life. I mean, someone actually loves me for me—ugly little old me. But then I thought, *Okay, I don't have to worry about making seating arrangements for her and her family of ten.*

A couple of days later, he called me, but I would not answer the phone and I told everyone to say that I wasn't home. I just didn't want to see him, and I didn't need the company. I had just found out that I was pregnant. Besides, I wasn't feeling well, but we did go to the movies with my brother and his wife. Bottom line I decided not to marry him. You see, I figured, if he loves me now, then he would love me next year and the year after that—and the year after that.

No one wanted to answer the door, and you know what? I don't blame them. Self is such a pain in the a—. However, the pain he is still my brother, and I can't leave him outside. Ouch, what was that? I felt a sharp pain in my lower right side. *Okay, this pain is not going away, and it's really starting to hurt. I'm going to take a shower, and if it continues, then I will head to the hospital.*

Badetta wasn't just my Lamaze partner, she was Beauty's daughter, my oldest niece, at least I think she is. I say that to say this. We are supposed to be eight months apart, but each year, she changes her age. To tell you the truth, I don't remember turning thirty. Maybe that was the year she actually turned thirty and said she was thirty-one. That reminds me, I need to call her to ask her how old she will be this year. This way, I will know how old I need to be. She was good though. She came to all of my Lamaze classes, she also kept us laughing by massaging my legs and saying crazy things. She was supposed to help me relax. Instead, she almost got us put out. I believe she was just as excited as I was in my becoming a mother.

"Who are you?"

"I'm your nurse, and this is the officer that will be placed outside your door. And the security guard will stand outside of the nursery. If you need anything, please don't hesitate to call. Oh yeah, you will have to come up with a password, so when you have visitors, we will know that they are coming for a visit and they are not the intruder. This password will have to change from day-to-day. We just don't want to take any chances."

I almost forget about that nutcase. The nurse was a lot nicer than that fool doctor who told me that since I never had a baby before, I wouldn't know if I was in labor or not. So I quickly told him that he would never have a baby, so he wouldn't know what labor was either.

Seventy-two hours later, weighing in at eight pounds ten ounces, Truth was here. They laid him on top of me, but I couldn't feel a thing, so I asked them to take him off me. He looked so gray. He looked like a little elephant, he was so big. When I was finally able to walk over to see my son, I had the police officer escort me, and the security guard was in place. I told them that they could remove the security at the nursery and replace him with the police officer. I told them that I would be okay. When I did see my baby for the first time, he was in this little bed with lights all around him. The nurse explained that he had jaundice. That night, they made the happy parents a lobster dinner. I thought he would have showed up to see his son, but he didn't. I just threw the dinner away. Yes, the lobster dinner went into the trash. Not because he was a no-show, but because I am allergic to seafood.

I stayed in the hospital for almost two weeks with the police by our side. They said the baby could go home, but I had to stay because I had a fever. I told them, "My baby does not go anywhere without me." Tango came to visit me in the hospital, but I had to ask him to leave and not come back. I'm sorry, but I had just had a C-section, and he kept the women and me laughing so hard that we were crying because we were in so much pain from the C-sections. Well, it was time to be discharged, and instead of leaving from the front of the hospital, we had to leave from the freight elevator and out the back just in case this nutcase discovered I delivered the baby and knew I was being discharged. Shoot, I had plans of leaving the hospital from the front in a limo and having it videotaped, but because of this crazed chick, I couldn't do it.

It was so nice to be at home and in my own bed. I couldn't wait to see my baby in his new cradle I bought him. This was top-of-the-line, it was the one that they give away on that game show—you know, the white oval-shaped porcelain cradle with the scalloped edges and brass knobs. It was beautiful, and nothing was too good for the Golden Child. That's what my family had started calling him because he had everything a baby could ever need. I came into some money from the accident I was in last year, so I was able to do this.

My Momma Didn't Raise No Fool

Wait a minute, someone was knocking at my door. "Who is it?" It was Tango. "Okay, wait a minute, I'm getting the baby ready for bed. What's up?"

"He's here." "He who"

"Him who that's who"

"You want him to come up?"

"No, I don't want him coming up here. I just put the baby down for the night, and I don't know where he's been or who he was with, so you can tell him to turn right around and go down the steps."

Knock, knock, knock!

"What! Are they stupid?" I asked Tango to tell him to go away.

"What do you want? You want to see who?" I asked. "First of all, you don't deserve to see anyone, and second, how did you know to come by and see the baby? How did you know we were even home from the hospital? Oh, my bad, I forgot. Now I remember who you are, you are the man with the wife. And don't start telling me some sh—about you not being married because I heard it all before. I'm not going to be mean. There is the bathroom, go in there and wash your hands and put one of these hospital gowns on." I wasn't playing. "Before you or anyone else comes in here, they have to put one of these gowns on, especially you."

And I didn't care how he looked at me, either he did it or he would have to leave. It was as simple as that. "Now you can go downstairs, and we will be down in a minute."

You would have thought I was calling the enforcers: Tango, Phar, Self, Melo, and Quick. These were my brothers, and they sat downstairs and waited by the front door just in case this guy wanted to act a fool up in here.

Sugar came by to visit, and I thanked her for the thumbs-up. I could have been home watching a rerun of "Good Times" that night. You wouldn't believe what this guy put me through tonight. I also reminded her of those two guys we went out with whose license plates our brothers wrote down as we drove off. Then there was this one I dated that was a complete jerk, Xerox was his name. He was a handsome guy, but I didn't know if he was dating me or my brother Quick. They were always together. That's why I swore off dating any of my brothers' or sisters' friends—because they end up dating my entire family. And sometimes your family can be in your business.

Well, I'm glad I stopped dating him because they were in a business I didn't want any part of. Listen to this. One Sunday morning, I was getting ready for church, and Xerox, came to my house, banging on my front door, waking up the other people in my house, demanding someone come and speak to his mother and explain to her that they were not selling drugs with her son from their house. He also wanted me to come to his house to explain to his mother that I didn't come to his house this morning wanting or needing to buy drugs. Now you know something was wrong, so I told him that when I finished getting dressed, I would walk around the corner.

When I got to his house, he opened the door. His mother, stepfather, and this man that lived across the street from him named Mr. B swore to his mother that he saw me that very morning asking him who could I get drugs from. I was upset. For one thing, I was at home getting dressed for church, and second, I had to remind Mr. B that I didn't speak to him because he propositioned me and I had cursed his a—out. He then remembered that it wasn't me that he saw, it was supposed to be my sister Coffee he said he saw. I told his mother that I was sorry that we had to meet under these circumstances and that I was running late for church. My favorite aunt had asked me to come to her church, so I did. I even joined the choir, at least until I heard them sing "Amazing Grace."

Anyway, as I started to walk down the block, Xerox came running after me, saying that his mother would like for me to come to dinner. I was so angry that I told him no and that I didn't want to speak to him anymore. I mean, he stood right there and never opened his mouth to tell his mother that I wasn't that type of person. I knew this guy from high school, but we never spoke. He was on the basketball team, and I was on the booster squad. The booster squad is second to the cheerleaders. It was like being a backup singer for Patti Labelle when you really wanted to be Patti Labelle, but I guess everyone had their moments in high school.

This guy was going down the wrong path with Quick. Just a couple of nights later, Quick, Xerox, and, I believe, this other guy who they claim was his cousin Blu (because he drove a blue Cadillac) came running around the corner after we heard gunshots. Instead of them telling us what was going on, they ran inside the house. The next morning, Quick sent his girlfriend Newport and their son to her mother's house. They just left the rest of us sitting in my house, without a clue as to what was happening and by that afternoon, we heard one of the guys in the neighborhood had gotten shot, and then things all started to make sense. But the guy that was shot said that it wasn't them that did the shooting and that someone else did it. Quick said they had just witnessed the shooting and ran—you think? Mind you, Quick is the same guy that put drugs into his son's Pampers and traveled to the Carolinas. He even had the nerve to have his own mother in the car with him during one of those trips. This guy was unbelievable.

Then there was this one time I was going into the basement to get my laundry when I saw Popcorn jump on the bed. Quick turned his back, and his friend the little weasel just sat there like he was watching TV. I asked what was going on, and of course, they said nothing. So I went outside, only to learn they were mixing up their drugs. I was also told Popcorn was paid to hide the stuff if anyone came downstairs. Now why would he do this here? Why would he do it at all? He could have rented an apartment and had his shop set up there, but instead he decided to do his business in the house we grew up in—the house the neighborhood grew up in my mother's house.

"Look, it's getting late, and I have to put the baby to bed. Do yourself a favor and don't come around here in this condition again, okay?" I mean, this guy was at least 80 proof—of what, I don't know. I wonder how he even made it home that night, but that was no concern of mine. I didn't care what he was doing or who he was doing anymore. A couple of days had gone by and I hadn't heard from him. Either he forgot about us, or he didn't know what to say when he called. One day, he must have gotten up the nerve to stop by, and surprisingly, he was sober. He was even talking like he had sense, but I found out later that he ran into my sister, and she had told him that he should stop by and see his son again. We sat up most of the night, talking about what had happened and what plans were to be made about future visits and what role he would play in his son's life, if any.

A few days would go by before I would see him again. This time, he did not come alone. He was with his father, and he told me that his father would like to see the Truth, only Truth was asleep. I told him that it would be best to call first. They left after he asked if we were okay, but not if we needed anything.

I almost thought he cared, but what on earth was on his mother's mind? He showed up one cold day in hell because that's the relationship that his mother and I had, at least that's the way I thought she felt about me in reference to us seeing one another or me seeing her son, And it was a cold day in hell. There she was, sitting in their car, wanting to see Truth. I told him that she could come in, but he told me that she could not walk up the steps, so I dressed Truth warmly. He was two months old, and it was the middle of February. I took him out into their car, and instead of her saying how beautiful he was, she remarked on how big his eyes were and the fact that he had reddish brown hair and freckles.

My mama didn't raise no fool. She was trying to see if he looked like her son, but instead, what she did notice was that he had a much lighter complexion than me, and it only took one remark in order for me to realize that it was time to take him inside. And that remark was that his ears weren't dark, so his complexion probably would not change. You see, that's one of the first things that some black people look at once a baby is born. If the ears are dark, then they figure the baby's complexion will be dark. Suffice to say, his ears were dark, but that was due to the dead skin on his ears, which some babies have. As a matter of fact, he had a lighter complexion than her son, and for her information, we have a beautiful rainbow of brown color in my family.

Why in the world did he leave me in the car alone with his mother? Did she tell him before they came to my house that she needed to talk to me alone? It took her no time to ask me if I had any other children. I let her know that I had custody of my niece and nephews. She also wasted no time in telling me again that he had a wife and that he didn't have a lot of money. I quickly told her that I owned this house and that I had my own money. I also told her that he was welcome to visit his son anytime he wanted to, but my son will not want for anything, at least from her. Before you knew it, he was opening the car door. He must have figured out that it wasn't the best thing to do; leaving us in the car too long together.

I got out and gave him this look as if to say, "She's your mother, not mine." But, all due to respect, I kept my mouth shut, but not my mind. I was able to have my thoughts, and oh boy, was I letting her have it. But Truth was waiting, and I was a mother now, and all that tit-for-tat stuff was behind me, at least for now—or was it? Four months had gone by, and our relationship was getting better. He was coming by and spending a lot of time with Truth, especially when I was sick. Truth needed a bath, and I couldn't give him one, so he decided to get some baby oil and a piece of cloth, and wipe him down, and by the time he was finished, my baby looked like a new penny. He was so proud of caring for

Truth that he had to run downstairs to tell my mother how he was taking care of Truth. Little did he know that while he was downstairs, I was upstairs, wiping off some of the baby oil. I thought the baby was going to slip through my hands. Okay, he did a good job, but not a good job in keeping his women in line.

Those women are either stupid, dumb, or hooked on phonics. Why would you knock on the door of the woman's house you suspect your man to be at and ask to see him? I answered the door that morning and when I saw him later I told him that this woman was asking for him and that he needed to explain who she was. So after speaking with her, he told me that she was his parole officer and that his mother told her that he was no longer living at her home. So she brought him his suitcase, and said he was in violation of his parole. but that wasn't the truth. I later found out from his best friend that this chick was from Staten Island and was at my home the night before when Freeport answered the door, but Freeport didn't know we were home at the time, so she told her that we were not home, and she left, but before she left, she said she was his girlfriend and that she would be at his mother's house waiting for him.

Freeport told me that someone was looking for him, but she thought we were out that night. It only took a minute for me to get my clothes on and head for the boulevard. Freeport went with me but we didn't find her, but I was told by my friends on the boulevard that there was an old woman fitting her description driving up Farmers boulevard. What I mean by old was that she was as old as her birthday and as old as my birthday too. She had to be at least forty-five years old looking like she was going on fifty, and he was thirty-three going on stupid. To top it off, another woman even older than her was also in the car, but this woman fit the description of his mother. When I got back to the house, the only brilliant thing he thought should come out of his mouth was a marriage proposal again, and again I turned him down—and for the same reason. I was pregnant again and was tired of hearing his stories. He needed to give me truth, and at this point, all I wanted was Justice.

And Justice for All

And here she came, weighing in at nine pounds five ounces. Justice, my beautiful little girl, or was it another boy? After being in labor for twenty-four hours and having been given an epidural, I'm surprised I even knew my name. Coffee and her boyfriend were there at the hospital with me. I was sweating so much that Coffee began wetting paper towels so I could suck on them, and her boyfriend patted my face with dry towels. The nurse told me that they were trying to let me have this baby naturally. Now who asked her to play God with my body? I had enough. I wanted to get this over with, especially when I heard this one woman holler. We thought it was because she was delivering her baby, but the nurse told us that the woman was just told that her baby had died. *Well, why don't they remove her from this floor?* I thought to myself, *They should put her on another floor. This way, she won't have to see everyone else with their babies.*

Coffee and her boyfriend went downstairs to get something to drink and to smoke a cigarette, but by the time they came back upstairs, they were wheeling me into the delivery room. I was maxed out to ten centimeters, and the baby still did not come. Coffee was told by the nurse they had to leave the floor, and of course. Coffee got upset. She started yelling at the nurse and told them that she had every right to be upstairs with me, just like everyone else was with their family members going into the delivery room. As her voice got louder, more nurses came out to see what was going on. Her boyfriend even tried to calm her down. He was a nice-looking guy, but he was real slick. He drove a taxi cab and could hardly speak English. He told us he was from Pakistan, but who cared? I just wanted to have this baby. I wonder if I still owe him cab fare for driving me to the hospital. I wanted to ask her where do she meet these men, but I was a little busy.

Among all the boyfriends she had, there was one guy I really disliked. He was in the service and thought he was *it*, but then she did have this one boyfriend. I thought he was perfect. She married him, and they had one daughter. It was a shame that they didn't stay together. *No*, they did not divorce, and you should know better than that. You know black people don't divorce, they just live with other people's husbands and wives.

Boy, the labor room was crowded, I didn't know there were supposed to be so many people in here. I guess some were medical students.

They put this cold stuff on my belly and draped this blue curtainlike thing in front of me. They also tried to give me anesthesia, but it wasn't working. And I kept telling them I was choking, and I needed some air, but the moron of a nurse told me as long as I could breathe, I was okay. A few minutes later, I heard a cry, and then I felt very cold. One nurse stood next to me and asked me if I was okay, so I told her that I was cold and my body felt numb. I was told they would be cleaning me up and taking me into the recovery room in a few minutes, so I just needed to hold on. The next thing I noticed, one of the nurses was standing at the door of the delivery room and another was leaving the delivery room. I yelled, "Wait, I didn't see my daughter." This one nurse turned and stated, "You didn't see your baby yet?" And another nurse asked, "How do you know you had a girl?" I told her, "I asked God for a girl, and he gave her to me." And besides, I already have a son at home.

I couldn't believe it. I really had a daughter this time. He did it, we did it. I thought he would have given me another boy. I thought I was going to have sons because I have a lot of brothers, and Popcorn had given birth to a little girl just a month ago. You may think it was a silly, but I stopped speaking to Popcorn. And I didn't want to see or hold her baby. I thought it was unfair to bless her with a baby girl when she clearly wanted a boy, and I thought the opposite was going to happen to me. I almost forgot. If I didn't say it before, I'm saying it now, "*Thank you, God.*"

Maybe if I had thanked God sooner, I would have been able to get out of my bed to go and see my baby instead of the nurses bringing Justice to me. You know, they wouldn't let me hold her, I guess it was because I had a fever. Well, you know what? I was tired of lying in this bed, and as soon as Beauty came to visit, we took a walk over to the nursery to see Justice. I was told that because of my fever I should stay in bed. If my fever hadn't broken in two days, it wasn't going to break. Besides, this little walk to the nursery would be good for me.

I know everyone believes they have the prettiest baby in the nursery, so I just had to point out Justice. But Beauty told me that I was wrong, not to say that I didn't have a beautiful baby, but I was looking at the wrong baby. I told her I should know what my daughter looked liked. Then she pointed out the name over the baby's head, and she was right, I was looking at the wrong baby. My daughter was on the other side. You know it didn't dawn on me that the baby that I was looking at was wrapped in a blue blanket and was a boy, and the baby that Beauty was looking at was wrapped in a pink blanket with my name over her head and was a girl. This was so embarrassing, a mother not being able to tell her baby from another baby, hmm.

Later that evening I decided to walk back to the nursery. Only this time, there was another new mother looking at her baby. I couldn't get over the fact that there was another baby that looked just like my Justice, and as I shook my head, a nurse came to the door and said to me that she was wondering when I was coming back to the nursery today. She wanted me to meet the other mother standing there. She was the mother of the infant baby boy I had mistaken as Justice. I didn't tell her that I was down here earlier and picked out the wrong baby. Anyway, the nurse thought it would be nice for us to meet, being that the babies looked so much alike. She also made a stupid joke like, "Wouldn't it be funny if they had the same fathers." Well, the other mother thought it was funny and laughed, but little did she know that was an insult, so I replied that the joke would be on her because I wasn't the one that was married, and I left the window.

I guess the nurse felt bad about what she said, so she came to my room with a picture of herself and of both infants in her arms and wrote on the bottom of the picture "which is which," and in the back was the identification of which baby was on the left and which baby was on the right.

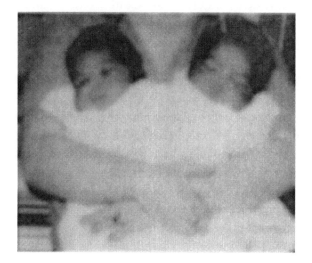

To this day I still get it wrong. The nurse told me that she gave a copy of the picture to the other mother as well. The other mother said that she would like to stay in touch with me, so she wrote her name, address, and phone number on the back of the picture. I thought that was odd, why would she want to stay in touch with me? She told me that she has a ten-year-old son at home and that she too wanted a girl. I told her to take care and that I will stay in touch.

The next day I was ready to go home, but the doctors told me that I couldn't because I still had a fever. I told him that I had a son at home who needed me and that my mother and her sisters were nurses and they knew how to care for me, so I discharged myself against doctor's orders. My mother, Beauty, and Truth came to pick me up from the hospital. I missed my little Buddha. He was the cutest little bald-headed baby I ever did see and he was very fat. He did look like the little boy from the movie the *Golden Child*. I was extremely tired when I got home and was happy to see my own bed. If you ever spent any time in the hospital, you know what I mean. Those hospital beds can leave your bottom sore.

Three months later, Justice started throwing up, and she had a fever. I asked my mother to watch Truth because I was going to take Justice to the hospital. The doctor decided to change her milk and said she would be fine, so I did and she was, at least for a couple of months. This time she got this rash, so the doctor told me to use oatmeal soap, which seemed to have worked at that time. Later that evening I came across the picture from the hospital and decided to give her a call to see how the woman from the hospital and her baby were getting along, and the funniest thing had happened during our conversation. She told me she had to take her baby to the hospital because he was allergic to the milk and had a fever. At first I thought nothing of it. Some babies are allergic to milk and have fevers, but when she told me that he also had a rash, I thought this isn't funny anymore. There are too many things to consider:

1. Staying in labor for twenty-four hours when I knew I was supposed to have a C-section.
2. A woman losing her baby and remaining on the maternity floor.
3. Coffee and her boyfriend being told they had to leave the floor while other people continued to have family and friends with them.
4. The labor and delivery room being crowded with extra medical staff.
5. I had to ask to see my baby after she was born.
6. The door to the delivery room was ajar as a nurse left.
7. Not recognizing my baby in the nursery.

8. The nurse saying it was a good idea for both mothers to meet and then taking a picture with the babies and asking, "Which is which?"
9. Both babies being allergic to their milk, then it was the fevers and then the rash.
10. And to top it off, the conversation ended when the mother of the infant told me that she was going to send her six-month-old infant to a poor country where there is so much political violence. I believe she is Haitian and so am I. I mean my dad is from Haiti, and you are what your father is.

I knew something was wrong, but I couldn't prove it. Did I give birth to twins? Did the hospital take one and give it to the woman who was screaming because her baby had died and it was the hospital's fault that her baby died? Did her husband find out about the babies? I don't know. All I do know is that my children's father side of the family has multiple sets of twins, and in each set there is a boy and a girl. My god, his sister has a set of twins, a boy and a girl. Yes, he does have a sister. As a matter of fact, he has two sisters and a brother.

Two years later, Justice had a nasty little fall on the school bus and hurt her bottom lip, so I took her to the hospital where they said she had to have surgery because her lip kept bleeding and was not healing on its own. The day before her surgery, she had to have her blood drawn. Justice did such a good job that the technician gave her a lollipop and said that he kept still today and that he did better today than he did yesterday. I pulled her hat off and told the tech that she was a girl and we were not in the clinic yesterday. The technician said that he could have sworn a little boy had come into the clinic yesterday with the same problem and was scheduled for surgery. I thought that I had put the twin theory behind me, but I guess it will always be there, or will I find closure?

I decided to get a copy of my hospital records, and believe it or not, they were all blacked-out sonograms. I later asked for my hospital records and was told that my records were destroyed, because the hospital only kept records for seven years. I was also told that the hospital keeps the medical records of infants for twenty-one years so I asked for Justice records; now I have to wait and see.

Is this a nightmare, or is this one of those lifetime stories where I'm the main character. I spoke to my father and asked him to help me since the baby was supposed to be sent to the country that he was from. Maybe he knew someone there that could look around, see if anyone knew of an infant being sold, or even an infant was brought there without their biological parents within the last couple of months. I guess he didn't believe me. I also told the story to my mother, and she told me that most black babies look alike and that we all have a twin somewhere. When I told the rest of my family and friends, I guess they thought I was out of my mind, especially my children's father. He looked at me as if I was losing my mind. Maybe I should have listened to his mother and not get involved with him. I guess she knew him better than I did, but it wasn't her place to tell me to have an abortion, and she was out of place when she told me, "If I didn't put my a—up to him, then I would not have gotten f—."

I, for the first time in my life, was speechless. I didn't know if I was in shock or in disbelief because this was supposed to be a church-going woman, and to say those things to me, I wanted to curse her out, but I couldn't. She was my children's grandmother and his mother, and of course when I told him what she said, he told me that his mother would not say something like that. I guess he thought her mouth was like a prayer book. At this point all I wanted was some answers. I didn't want to hear from anyone, especially from him. He knew I was angry. He was supposed to bring some Pampers with him, but of course, he didn't. And I was down to my last pack. Popcorn wanted to go food shopping and pick up a few things, but I didn't know when she said pick up a few things that. It was exactly what she did, and she showed me how. We would go into the pharmacy to purchase something, then go to the back of the store to pick up a pack of Pampers. (Fortunately, they had the double packs of Pampers because they were using them double as fast.) Then we would hold the receipt in one hand and act like we were counting our change while talking to each other. Next we would walk right out the store and right through the front entrance. We made it look as if we purchased everything we had. This happened with her for a while. I couldn't do it anymore. She started going to other stores and take clothes, baby bottles, pork chops, you name it she was able to get it. She was so good she even walked out the store one day with a new stroller. I remember one day while walking to the park I was kidding her about her baby stroller. The wheels were rolling the opposite direction of which she was pushing, making it look as though the stroller had a mind of its own. I thought she was kidding when she said she was going to get her baby a new stroller, but like I said, the girl was good—she got that baby a new stroller.

I hadn't spoken or seen him for days, and when he did come back around, he came with this lame of a marriage proposal. I told him to forget it and to forget him. I think he should stop proposing to me. It seems as though every time he does, I am pregnant. *Yes, I'm pregnant again.* And again, I turned him down, and I told him that I didn't want to see him again, so he left, and I hadn't seen or hear from him for months, until my niece and nephew came from the store and told me they saw him on his way to my house driving a car with this older woman in it. He was heading in my direction. They believed it was his mother. He was coming by to tell me that his father had passed away. I thought, *Oh my god, that man meant the world to him, and I am so sorry for his loss.* He called my house later that afternoon and left a message with my mother to tell me about the arrangements for the wake and funeral. He wanted me and the children to come, so I called Tango, Phar, and Face to see if they would come with me. You know how it is when you go to a black person's funeral, all hell breaks loose.

I called his house and spoke to his mother. I told her how sorry I was about their loss and asked to speak to him. She said he was out with his cousin and she would give him the message. She told me the time and gave me the directions of the services for the next morning. Phar and Face came to take me to the services, so when we arrived, I went inside with the children and sat in the back pew. There were some people sitting just a couple of rows ahead of me, and one of them looked just like my children's father. Tango, Phar, and Face waited outside, and after a few minutes, I decided to join them since I didn't know anyone there, but by the time I got to the doors, two of his male cousins walked out behind me. One of them seemed to be very nice. He asked me if I needed any help. I told him that I was waiting for my children's father. He is the son of the deceased. He introduced himself to me while the other one who looked just like my children's father decided he wanted to play big shot and question me.

He had the nerve to ask me if his cousin knew I was coming, and to top it off, he asked if the baby I was carrying was his cousin's. This guy was nonstop. He saw my family standing below the steps, so he questioned who they were and asked which one was my boyfriend. I was so fed up with him that I had to put him in his place. I told him, "First of all, yes, he knew I was coming as if it was any of your business, and for your information, all three of these children are your cousins, and since you are all in my business, those three guys are my family they grew up with your cousin." He made me so mad, my children's father never questioned the paternity of our children, at least not to me. He knew better. I mean he knew I didn't sleep around and that's not how I rolled.

I guess the nice cousin saw I was getting a little agitated by the questioning and took me inside to meet the rest of the family. He introduced me to his mother who seemed to be very nice. She introduced herself as my children's cousin, and that was nice. It started to get late, and I couldn't wait for him so we left. Later that evening he called me and told me he heard we were there for the services, so he asked me if we would be there tomorrow for the funeral. I told him of course. He asked his mother what time was the funeral. She told him it was at 10:00 a.m.

The next morning, Phar drove us to the church, but when we arrived, this man on the street told us that everyone had already left. I was so angry. Phar said that he would take me home. I told Phar, "No, take me to his mother's house." Phar told me that I'm one crazy female. I said, "No, I'm one pissed-off pregnant woman who had just about had enough." When we arrived, his male cousin, the nice one, came out to meet us and brought us into the house and introduced us to the family, as family. It was a nice, I felt welcomed, but I was still upset. He also told me that my children's grandmother was in the kitchen and I could go in and see her. "No, maybe later." As I began to sit near the window, I saw their father getting out of the car talking to his cousin who was questioning me at the church. Before completely sitting, I noticed the woman sitting against the wall. I smiled and thought, *This is going to be better than I thought.* She was his current live-in, the same idiot that came to my house with his suitcase looking for him. I remember he told me she was his parole officer and his mother was putting him out because he was not staying at her house any more. Well, that turned out to be a lie. She was that old chick from Staten Island, so instead of sitting on the bench by the window, I asked Phar if I could sit in his seat because it would better for my back. I sat directly across from her, belly and all. I even spoke to her and said hello. (Do you think she was upset? Hmm.)

Okay, that was fun. Well, what do you know. Here he comes along with that a—hole cousin of his. I just wish he would say something stupid today. As he shook Phar's hand, he told me that he had just left my house. I couldn't help but look over at her as if to say, You see we aren't together anymore, and he's supposed to be living with you, but where did he just come from when he told her that he was walking to the store which is just around the corner." Okay, for real I'm here only to show my respects. This is not going to be another one of those black people funerals where a fight breaks out.

I was hoping he didn't ask, but the time has come, he asked the question, "Did you see my mother yet?"

"No, I didn't. I was waiting for you."

So we went into the kitchen, and lo and behold another surprise, his second wife was sitting at the table right across from his mother. You remember that crazy chick that threatened to take my baby from the hospital. I almost didn't see her because I was trying to hide my belly. You see, I didn't want his mother to see I was pregnant just in case she didn't know. I didn't want this to be the way she would find out, besides this wasn't the place. It was a small kitchen, but I guess it was enough space to hold his two female cousins, one standing at the stove and another cousin standing in the middle of the kitchen. Did they think it was going to be a show? His mother seemed to be very pleasant considering she didn't like me. From what I was told, she didn't like his wife either. He said she was young, immature, and he married her when he got out of jail. Yes, I said jail. Look don't play like you don't know, either the black man is six feet under or six years in. Either way as a black male, you have strikes against you. Just in his situation, he was batting more than Sammy Sosa:

He is African American
He has three children
He is on his second marriage and,
He doesn't have a job man

It didn't matter though. We were getting ready to leave, and if looks could kill, I would be dead twice over—one from his wife and one for the old chick sitting in the living room. Oh, I didn't tell you, his wife was no older than twenty. I guess he liked them in all decades, he himself was thirty five. He may not have thought I noticed, but I did. I saw his cousin pull him aside and whisper to him. Well, maybe it wasn't a whisper because I heard her say to him that he must have brass balls in order to have three women here, and I know she knew the tension that was brewing in the house.

It was time for us to leave when he pulled me aside and asked if I would be home, because he would like to stop by my house later that afternoon to talk and visit with the kids. I wanted to stay to see the rest of his family, or maybe just to stay long enough to see the expression on their faces when they saw all three of us in the same house without killing each other. Mind you, I never said we didn't want to, it's just that we didn't. He told me he had several sets of twins in his family and he wanted me to see them. I thought if you've seen one set of twins, you've seen them all, and what was so special about seeing these twins? I guess I didn't give up the possibility that I could have given birth to twins since they run so strong on his side of the family, but I was tired, and my feet was starting to swell so we left, of course without a scene.

An announcement was heard on the TV that HIV has infected another celebrity. I was shocked. I thought only gay people and people who did drugs had HIV. What was going on? This is a respectful man, he is not on drugs, and I don't think he is gay. So how did he contract the virus? That's when one and two made three. He had an affair with an infected person. Oh . . . my . . . god, what is going on? Think and think hard. I just left a funeral of my children's father where he had his ex-wife, his present girlfriend, and me. I can't do this. When he comes, I have to let him know that it is over and that I never want to see him again. This man could very well be carrying the virus and give it to me or have given it to me already. He has lied to me before. Shoot, what makes me believe that he is not going to lie to me if I ask him if he is infected.

I wonder if he is he willing to take a blood test. Okay, maybe it's time to use some muscle, either he gives up some blood or I will get it one way or another. Wait, forget him. I need to be tested, and so do my children. Okay, now breathe. What am I going to do if he comes tonight. I will remember that he just lost his father, but I need to think about me and mine. I can't see him anymore. He is too much of a risk, and he's not worth it. Besides he is doing his old girl, and I am going to do me and the kids. I felt really bad for him when he came into my bedroom. He looks as if the floor had fallen from underneath his feet. I felt like I was holding the rug at one end and pulling at the other, but I had to do it. I DON'T THINK WE SHOULD SEE EACH OTHER ANYMORE, and as for the kids, they would be fine and maybe better off at this point.

A Wise Man Once Said

I need to make decisions and need to have a clear head with no interruptions. In other words, I need to wise up and I did. Wise came in weighing eight pounds, eight ounces. He was the easiest baby I had ever delivered. He acted like he didn't want to come out, they actually had to pull him away from my body. He felt as if he was a blob of goo, he was so wet. I was in heaven, not because the delivery was over, but because the doctor asked me was I sure I wanted my tubes tied. If I could tie them myself, I would. He asked me if I was having any doubts, what did he think, I mean I had three babies, and all of them were C-sections. I'm not going through this again for nothing in the world or no one. I remember one time I asked him to have a vasectomy, he looked at me as if I told him I knew where *Bin Laden* was and didn't want the reward.

Well, that's it. What is done is done. Now I have three children of my own, my fifteen-year-old niece who we referred to as a Koala bear (because she was round and beautifully brown), and I also had two nephews that I am raising by myself, not to mention returning to college full time to get my degree. During the first couple of months, so many things were happening and not for the better. First, my niece decided she was grown since she had a baby. She had just turned sixteen and was visiting with her baby father's grandmother. You see the baby's father was not there because he was killed in a car accident way before we even knew she was pregnant. We heard that summer about a young man who was killed in a car accident in our neighborhood and that he was a friend of my niece and nephew, but what I did not know was how much of a friend he was to her. At least not until another niece came from the funeral and wanted to know why she didn't attend the services, after all she was his girlfriend. I wonder why she didn't go to the services, but she said nothing the whole time. I figured maybe she was in shock, so I left her alone.

She continued to get good grades in school and was coming home on time after school, so what was I worried about? I never had a problem with her before this, except the time when her father moved back into the neighborhood and wanted to build a relationship with her. I thought that would be a good idea. It seemed as though everything was working out fine, she continued to go to school and was about to graduate from the eighth grade, and she wanted to live with her father, and he wanted her to live with him. He had a two-bedroom apartment in the back of an alley. It sounds bad, but it was really a nice little place, besides I could check on her from time to time. To my surprise I found out her father had given her a key to their house, and she was letting herself in the house. She was alone after school, so what was he thinking? I know she was thirteen years old at the time, but the idea of walking through the alleyway by herself was unthinkable, so I spoke to him about that and suggested she come to my house after school and he could pick her up from there. I knew he didn't like the idea, but what other choice did he have? Well, he didn't, so she asked her father if she could go to a friend's house after school. He said it was okay, this way she could meet him at home when he arrived home from work. Well, how smart was he? Did he once think to check to see if her friend was a boy or a girl? Well, the friend turned out to be a boy rather a young man who was nineteen years old.

I guess she thought she was getting away with being an independent adult, or just being fast, but her actions slowed down. She started to visit us more and was very quiet, I mean more than usual. I was on my way to visit my sick aunt in the Bronx when another relative told us that Koala was raped last month by three boys—rather men, they were nineteen, twenty, and twenty-one. Well, I don't have to tell you the trip to the Bronx had to wait. I spoke to her mother and went to see my Koala at her father's house and told him what I was just told. When I went into her bedroom to talk to her, she admitted to the rape, so I took her to the hospital. This was one of the worst experiences I ever had to undergo. They called the social worker and started with the rape kit. I wanted to die for her. She was just a baby, so as I began to hold her hands as they examined her, I did not know what to feel—anger because of what was happening to this baby, or rage because of what they did to her.

Well, all the test results came back negative, and she was going to be fine. First thing, she was moving back home. Second, I made a few phone calls. First to arrive were my brothers, a few carloads of friends, her father, and myself. We drove through their neighborhood, and she pointed out one of the guys. Of course he got smart, so I punched him in the face, and we began to fight. From out of nowhere he did see my brothers. While we were fighting, she pointed out the house where they lived, and the other two boys were there. They came to the door and were grabbed and beat as well. One of them got away and brought back a gun, so we jumped in our cars, got home, and called the police.

Of course we attempted to press charges, but the DA told me that if Koala took the stand, they will tear her apart, and I knew she could not handle the questions, so what they did was warn the men not to have any contact with her. They could not come near our house or near her school, which was a little difficult. They lived near her school, and she was afraid to return to school, so we spoke to the school administrators to see if we could make other arrangements for her to finish out the school year from home assignments. We agreed that her work could be sent home, completed, and returned until she felt comfortable enough to return to school. She began to open up again after a month of isolating herself in the house. She began to go to the park. She hung out with her cousin, and her parents even began to see her more.

We were pleased to find out that with all of this conflict, she was continuing to get good grades and only needed to return to school in May to take her final exams. It was prom time that she attended and looked beautiful. She had two dresses, the one she wore to the prom, she was told not to remove the tags. She was also told not to sweat because it was going back to the store in the morning. The dress was purchased at one store in Green Acres Mall and returned to their other store at Queens Center Mall where her graduation dress was purchased. I mean exchange (Thanks, Popcorn) She looked beautiful. I know it was wrong, but I could honestly say that it wasn't me who did the exchange, but it was me who was very proud of her at graduation. Coffee attended the graduation ceremony, and if I do say so myself, she looked good. She had her hair done, her makeup looked tight, she started to look like the sister and mother I knew she could be. I know she was not ready, but this was her day, I mean their day together.

Well, the fall had arrived, and she attended one of the best high schools in Queens, John Bowne High School in Bayside. She had a few friends and continued to get good grades. She had started to put the past behind her until we heard of the accident. It was Thanksgiving, and I was seven and a half months pregnant. I was going food shopping and decided to take Koala with me so we could talk. She obviously was depressed about losing her boyfriend, besides it's been a while since it was just her and I spending time together. It was nice I got her to laugh a few times and told her that everything was going to be all right, so we returned home, put the grocery away, and she went upstairs with the rest of the kids. Later that night my mother and I were talking and laughing about something, and I needed Popcorn to hear this. She was still living in the basement, so when I heard the steps creak, I began telling her what we were laughing at. As the footsteps got closer and I saw the belly, we began to laugh harder because I told her she was following me this time being pregnant. But my laughter soon changed to horror, the belly did not match the face, it was Koala's belly.

I almost had a heart attack. I asked her to come close to me. I lifted her shirt, and there it was that black line down the middle of her stomach. I said, "Ma, this child is pregnant." So I called her mother and her father. Of course her mother arrived and was crying, and I said to myself, "Great, just what I needed, another baby. What the hell is she crying for!" I needed her support, not for her to act like a big baby, and when her father came, it was even worse. He made up his mind. She was going to the clinic in the morning and have an abortion. Well, I guess he told me, NOT. I told him, "First of all, it looks like she is at least four months pregnant, and second, this is her choice and her body. I or we cannot make a decision with a life and it may just cost her hers." So he suggested she went down south to live with his estranged mother who I didn't know and who if I can recall him saying Koala didn't want to be bothered with his mother because of the way she treated her when she visited them some summers ago. Of course he was angry, and he left stating he wanted nothing to do with her. Who cared? After all, it wasn't like I was asking him for anything. I just figured they had a right to know, forget him.

The next day I got her in to see my doctor because I had an appointment and explained the situation. She examined Koala and came out to talk to me. She informed me that Koala was afraid to talk to me. I asked her why. The doctor told me, "She is much farther along than I thought. She may deliver before Christmas." I couldn't believe it. What was I going to do? I wasn't prepared for this. I already have four children at home with my one on the way, and now her and her one will make seven. Damn, I only went shopping for one baby. I guess we will have to split the clothes or try and give her a baby shower, but this is so last minute.

I was surprised to come home from the doctor's office one evening to find Koala eating spicy chili that her father had brought her, I guess he came to his senses, or the thought of child support was beginning to enter his mind. That was going to be my next step. I knew chili was hot, but who would have thought she would have gone into labor. We arrived at the hospital, and they took us right to the labor and delivery room. She was really in labor, but she had not dilated. So we waited and waited but nothing. The nurses were about to change their shift when we were told it may help to have her walk through the halls. As we were walking, a nurse asked which one of us was in labor. We were both due. However, I was scheduled for a C-section because I was overdue. The doctors asked me to pick a day in January to have my baby. I thought about giving birth on the first, but my uncle passed away on that day ten years ago. The doctors told me if I didn't go into labor by the tenth, I would be scheduled for a C-section on January 17. I wanted to wait until she had her baby. You see, I knew I was going to be in the hospital for at least a week or two, and because this is her first baby, I figured she would need some help getting settled at home with her baby.

"Okay, it is time, just relax and everything will be all right. You want to squeeze my hand. Push, push, push again. Okay, stop pushing."

"I see the head, thank God because my feet are swollen. I'm hungry and it's a long drive back."

"Okay, one more time, push on the count of three . . . one, two, three push."

"I never saw anything like this before. I can see the baby coming, so this is what it is like to be in labor and to have a baby naturally. Wow, ten and ten, everything is here, fingers and toes, and so is she Luv."

They handed her to me, but I told them to give her to her mother. I needed to sit down, but before I did, I noticed the top of the garbage can moving. I am either really tired or this baby's father just witnessed the birth of his baby girl. Finally, I'm home and I can't wait to get into my bed.

Decisions, Decisions

"Why in the world are these kids up at this time of night, Ma." "Whatever it is, can it wait. I'm tired and I need some sleep."

But of course, Mommy told me anyway. These kids were in the attic fighting, jumping around, and throwing things. She even told me that Tango's son was so angry at Melo's son that he destroyed my baby clothes. Yes, the clothes I just brought. That is the final straw. This kid has got to go back to his mother. I told her I would keep him until she came out of her inpatient drug program, but damn, it has been four years, and if she don't come get him, I'm going to need a program. Besides, Tango was incarcerated, so I called his mother and asked her to come get him. She said she could not come for him because she is still trying to get her stuff together. How much more does she need to get together? She finished the program, found a job, and from what I understand, she is supposed to be making about $500 a week while I'm still on welfare with 6.5 children. Is she kidding or what?

Well, she didn't come, and there is nothing else I can do except take him to the authorities and let her know she can pick him up from there. So I called her, and I told her, "This is where he will be." I know Tango is going to be upset when he finds out, so I will explain everything to him when he calls. About an hour later, I went to the precinct and told the officers what the situation was. I gave them her phone number and figured they could deal with this. I'm tired, and when I say I'm tired, I was tired. They called her and said they spoke with someone, and that someone would give her the message. I was told that they would call social services, and he would be placed in care if no one came. It was hard, but I couldn't do it anymore so I left, but I hid around the corner in my car to see if she was really coming, and she did. Thank God I didn't want him to be sitting in a foster home. Bottom line, I would have taken him home, and knowing me I would have gone to family court on Parsons Boulevard the next day and filed for custody.

It seems to me that everybody is trying to get themselves together except me. I mean, I am always helping someone get their life together even if it's supposed to be for a little while, but it turns out to be longer than I expect. This being on welfare is not going to make it. I have to either find a job or return to school. Maybe Coffee can watch the kids, after all one of them is her granddaughter. What is wrong with me? I should have known she would not do it without me paying her. I remember the last time I asked her to watch her daughter so I could keep my face-to-face appointment at the welfare, and if you ever been to that place on Sutphin Boulevard, you would know that was no place for children. To tell you the truth, that was no place for me either. That's why I wanted to finish school, so I wouldn't need welfare. I was able to keep my appointment, and of course, I had to pay her. I couldn't get in the door fast enough before she started to complain about me taking so long. she *claimed* she had something to do. Who was she kidding? If I saw the worker within the first half hour, I was doing good, but as usual, I was there all morning.

Okay, my classes are going well. She starts school for teen mothers tomorrow, and I got all the kids in daycare. Life is going to be good, especially when she brings the baby in from visiting her great-grandmother. You see, after her baby was born, we took her and the baby to see his family just to let them know a part of him still exist, even though he is not here. Well, maybe he was in the delivery room. My first thought in the delivery room was to make another hole in the wall while trying to get out of here, but then I whispered, "Beautiful isn't she." I knew he was there, he helped her get through it, and I thanked him. Now I needed someone to help me get through the moment. This little woman (koala) never came through the door. I called up the street to the baby's great-grandmother's house to let her know it was getting late and she needed to get the baby ready for bed, and she needed to get ready for school. So I waited a half hour for her to take a five-minute walk home. I called a second time, and this time she told me she was at a party and was going to stay the night. I told her the party was over and she needed to come home and take care of her business. Well, she came home, and she brought someone with her and not Luv. I asked her where was Luv and who was this guy she was with. She told me Luv was at her family's house and that she was moving out.

At this point this person was not important, besides he looked a lot like her baby's father. It must have been his brother. She got a large trash bag and placed all their things in it.

That night I called the police and reported the situation, so they sent a car to my house and took the report. They told me they would go to their house and find out her story. However, they returned rather quickly, just to tell she was not there. I later found out that someone from that family took her to another relative's house, supposedly up Farmers Boulevard or over to Laurelton. Well, I didn't lose any sleep that night. Okay, maybe some sleep, after all she did have the baby with her. The next day some people I know, who knew we were looking for her, said they saw her come out of the store on Farmers Boulevard talking to some guy. Well, a week has gone by, and I just about had enough, I already reported this to the police. I have to study for my finals, and I need to go back to the welfare this time for a one-shot deal.

A one-shot deal is when you present your outstanding bill to the worker and ask for assistance in paying your bill. I hope you don't think it's that easy. You also need collateral. Like my house, they placed a lien on my house, so if I sell my house, they are guaranteed payment from the sale, either that or go without lights, and I couldn't do that. My mom, my son, and I are asthmatics, and we use a nebulizer machine, so I had no other choice, besides where was I going to get $6,000 to pay that bill. How did it get so high? Why wasn't it shut off already? Well, seven brothers and sisters each with their own families, some with ready-made families, cousins, friends, and neighbors all coming and going, and some not paying bills; that's how the bill got high. They were just saving their money to get their own place. The slickest thing was to put the bill in someone else's name whenever it gets too high, and I guess by now they caught on.

Finally the letter from the Department of Social Services, I wonder how much of the bill they are going to pay, hopefully all of it. What the hell, they have got to be kidding. How in the hell are they charging me with child abuse? They might take all the children. Ain't . . . no . . . way they are coming in here to remove any of these kids. They would have to kill me first. This report is stating I neglected my nieces, I failed to provide food and shelter for them, and I verbally abused them. So I take it her so-called other family was able to convince Koala to have me charged just so she could hang in the streets and they could keep the baby. How stupid is she! I know they miss their loved one, but this was not the way to do things. I called Coffee, and I called her father. He acted like he didn't have a clue as to what I was saying. Okay, I got no support from him, but I know my sister will help me. She won't let them take these kids. You know they were separated for years, and they deserve each other. She didn't want to help me either, and she knew what I was talking about. It was almost as if she helped her file the papers I asked both of them in all of the years (eleven to be exact) that I had taken care of their daughter. Had they ever known me to neglect her or abuse her? Shoot, most people thought she was my biological daughter, and I treated her as if she were mine. I remember the day when her mother wanted some money and I didn't have any, so she threatened to take her out of the house, so I gave her some money, but that would be the last time I went to court and gained custody of her. So when she came back for more money or more threats, I would have had something for her, and like clockwork, she did come back, this time I had my papers. She threatened to take her out of the house, but when she found out she could not, she was furious. For one she wanted to know how the court gave me custody, and all I can say is go figure.

Anyhow, when she finally came by the house, I let her have it. We argued and I threw every ugly word and thought at her from being unfit, to trash, even a druggie, you name it. I said it. I couldn't believe it. I was on my own, and I could lose everything. Yes, these children are everything to me, and no one else gives a damn. I wanted her out of my face, I wanted to kill her, but she's not worth it. My first step in this fight was to write to Albany and question the allegations. Second, if they were going to charge anyone with abandonment, then it would need to be her parents, after all they left her with a seventeen-year-old, still in high school. I even had proof I was able to register her in public school and attended all parent-teacher meetings. I explained to them how she was raped while in the care of her father, and how she was seven and a half months pregnant when I found out. So if they wanted a fight, then a fight is what they will get, but what they will not get are these kids.

Well, it's finals time, and being a full-time student at a junior college is rough. I guess it's going to be a full investigation since I haven't heard anything yet. Well, I better get a lawyer because legal aid won't help, and Coffee coming by the house didn't help. You would have thought she would have had the sense to stay away from me. I was so mad I could have scratched her eyes out, but today I had to take the kids to daycare and walk from Linden Boulevard to Merrick Boulevard to catch the bus to school. It wasn't even 8:00 in the morning, and the morning felt long. Okay, what am I going to do? I'm going to take this one exam, then I am going to stop pass my friend's house to pay my respects to her family, and finally, I'll get some rest before I pick up the kids. I have this throbbing pain on the right side of my head, and my fingers have been tingling a bit. Maybe this is a sign that I'll hear from Albany today, and then all of this will pass. Well, it didn't pass, but I almost did.

I was lying on the sofa when I thought I heard my mom ask what time was I going to pick up the kids. She kept saying the same thing over and over and over again. My goodness, didn't she hear me the first time? Answer to that question, NO. She didn't. As a matter of fact, I wasn't saying anything out of my mouth. It was all in my head. I thought I was moving my lips, but nothing was coming out, maybe my ears are clogged. As a matter of fact, I could not move my body, I thought that I was sitting up, but I was just lying there. I couldn't move. God, what was happening to me. I was having a TIA (transient ischemic attack), in other words a ministroke. They rushed me to the hospital and sent me home hours later with my mouth twisted and numbness on the right side of my body. That night my hands and feet started to turn inward, so back to the hospital I went. This time they sent me home with medication and no memory of who I was, where I was, or who were the people in the house.

Who I did know were my children, but if my kids' father had walked up to me, I would not have known who he was. This lasted for about six months, and all I could do was pray because something wasn't right. School was put on hold, and the people in this house helped with the kids; and me, I worked on me. I slept in the living room with my mother because I was afraid of being by myself, afraid of not waking up, I was afraid of me. So I made a promise to God, and that's one person I would not forget. "God, if you can get me to feeling not afraid and okay again, then I will forgive those who sinned against me." I walked out of the bathroom and down toward my bedroom when I heard Coffee in the living room talking to my mother. I looked at her, and she looked at me, and then everything came back to me the very minute she asked me how I was feeling. Just then, school, my family, Albany, and everything else came back, including the anger. I wanted to continue the argument, but I didn't know where to begin or what was said the last time I saw her. But I couldn't, I made a promise to God, and I was going to keep it.

He Is the Father

Beauty called me today and couldn't wait to tell me who she saw. She said he wanted to get in touch with me and that he was happy to hear that we had another son. How did he know we had another son? I bet he went to the beauty parlor and spoke to the godmother. Well, it wouldn't hurt for him to see his children. To tell you the truth, it would be nice to see him. I wonder if he looks the same, you know four years can change a person. I know it changed me. Well, at least God did.

Badetta saw him standing at the bus stop on 179th Street and gave him a ride around the way. My mom and I were watching all the kids from the picture window in front of my house. They were playing in the front yard when they pulled up. I asked her, "Do you think he would recognize his kids?" I figured there are so many kids out there he probably won't recognize them. I started to walk away from the window when I heard Truth ask, "Who was that man?" Leave it to Justice to say, "That's Daddy, stupid."

Well, I guess he did know his children. He came into the house carrying Wise, with Justice and Truth not far behind him. Damn, he looks good, but I can't let him know that. I wonder how I look to him. There seems to be no signs of me having a ministroke. I lost some weight, but not a lot. He kissed my mom on the cheek and asked if we could talk. Damn, he could have said hello first. As he started up the stairs, I told him we could talk in the back room, which was now my bedroom. You see, the rule in this house was if you leave the house for more than thirty days, then you lose your room. Fortunately for me, almost everybody had already moved out of the house, and the only people still living in the house was my mom who had the master bedroom on the second floor and Tango had the front room on the first floor, right off the living room. Everyone thought it was the best room in the house, but I never did.

For one, whenever someone knocked at the front door, the person who slept in that bedroom was the one expected to get out of their nice warm bed and get the door. For two, there was no privacy. Whenever someone had company in the living room, it was as if they were sitting on your bed. My nephew had the second room on the third floor next to Coffee's old bedroom. Justice had the small room on the second floor with the antique mirror attached to the wall. Next door to my mom and down the hall from Justice was Truth and Wise who were next to the bathroom.

Doc's kids and Newport were living in the basement apartment. It had its own bathroom, entrance, and stories. When I say stories, I mean if ever there was a place that had good stories, it would be that basement. If it could talk, it would tell you all its secrets. It would tell you about all the money, the drugs, and jive talk that passed through there from all the aunts, uncles, cousins, nieces, nephews, grandparents, and friends. I almost forgot my bedroom was on the first floor right off the dining room, near the kitchen, and in front of the walk-in pantry, which used to be a bathroom. And around the corner from the pantry was the back room that had an exit. That room was the room my mother's sister was living in after it was decided by my mother's oldest sister, the matriarch of the family. She lived in the Bronx. I know, what nerve, but who was going to tell her no. She was the boss. I wanted to tell them no I could not care for her because I just had a TIA, but I couldn't. I loved her even though I was accused of taking her money and abusing her, but that's another story in itself.

APS, CPS, PMS

Someone called Adult Protective Services (APS) on me. It was no secret of who it was, but I had every I dotted and every T crossed, besides I had a home health aid there five days a week to take care of my aunt because I was in school. I also had the kids to take care of and my mom. When the APS came to the house, they found everything in order. I had every receipt for every dime spent on her, so the case was unfounded, but that didn't stop the calls except this time it was to Child Protective Services (CPS). The police came to my house several times stating that a call came through their office that stated I was abusing Justice and my other children, but because they did not know the names of my other children, I figured out who made the calls. CPS and the police came so often that I started asking them how were their families. They said everyone was doing just fine. One officer went so far to say that his mother-in-law was coming for a visit and you know how that is.

I even saw them on the streets, and they asked me how were the kids. After a few more calls and the middle-of-the-night visits, all they found were my children sound asleep and the house was quiet. They said that they were going to make a note of this and inform CPS of all the calls.

CPS came to the house anyway because that was the procedure, and what they found was Tango burning hot dogs on the grill, the kids running around, my mother and aunt sitting in the yard, and the rest of us playing cards. It was written as unfounded and probably a family dispute. The worker stated the anonymous calls were being made without substantial-enough evidence. The worker stated they had to act on the call because they were being made so frequent. I informed the worker about the APS case and told them it was probably stemming from that. The CPS worker contacted the APS worker and confirmed what I was telling her. The case was closed.

The calls eventually stopped, and some family members stopped speaking to each other, even those who had nothing to do with the situation. What bothers me the most is the thought of some family members believing I would do something to hurt my aunt. It even got to the point where some were taking sides. This side of the family wasn't speaking to that side of the family, and that side of the family wasn't speaking to this side of the family. It was ridiculous. She is one of my favorite aunts, to tell you the truth they were all my favorite aunts. You couldn't help but love them. I just wish I had the opportunity to have known them all. You see my grandparents had sixteen children, but I only knew ten of them, not including my mother. About four years before she got sick, my aunt and my brother-in-law gave me $5,000 to buy a car. I promised to repay them back, but he told me that it was for me because I was raising his daughter, and my aunt said it was for taking care of her sister, my mother. Come to find out they got together and decided to give me the money. What could I say, but thank you.

My first car was a Ford Tempo. It was my real first car, and it was beautiful and black, and it was all mine, at least for a little while. Why did I have to go there? This just brought back memories. I remember the day he spoke to his mother and she told him that his father needed him to come to her house and do something for him, so he asked me if he could use my car to go see his father. I knew his father wasn't well, so I told him he could use the car to go see his father. Three hours had passed and he had not returned. I was hoping that everything was okay, so I waited another hour before I called his friend to see if he had heard from him. He told me that he left his house about an hour ago and told him that he was heading back to my house, only he never arrived.

The next morning he still had not returned, so I decided to call his mother's house to see if everything was okay. She told me that he was not there and that I should not have given him the car because he does not have a license. Well, she could have fooled me. He would often come to my house driving his father's car, and several times, he would drive her back and forth to Brooklyn to take her to church and to visit her family. So, no, I didn't know that he did not have a driver's license.

I started to call the police to make a police report and tell them that he stole my car, but I couldn't because I gave him permission to use the car. The only thing I could report is him missing and never returning after he asked to borrow the car. I called his friend who told me that my car was up Farmers Boulevard and Linden somewhere wrapped around a fire hydrant. I asked Tango if he could go and see if he sees my car and bring it back to me if it's even mobile. As I was talking to Tango, he came walking through the door without saying a word. He looked at me and I looked at him. Tango asked him where did he leave the car. He told him up Farmers Boulevard and continued to walk into the bedroom. I got the keys from him and gave them to Tango.

By now I just wanted to hit him with whatever I could get my hands on. He made me so mad. He had the nerve to say to me that the only thing I care about is that car and that I didn't even ask him how he was doing. Now how in the hell was I supposed to know that something was wrong with him, especially after he came walking through the front door as if nothing was wrong. I asked him what did he mean by that. That's when he told me that the car was in the parking lot at Green Acres Mall when someone hit the car and kept going. He said he didn't know anything had happened to the car until he saw a police officer asking who was the owner of the car. Then where is the accident report and how does he explain how the car moved from Green Acres Mall to Farmers and Linden Boulevard. Why didn't he just confess and tell me the truth that he was drinking and driving and ran into a fire hydrant. The first thing out of my mouth to him was, "And you walked away from the accident." If looks could kill, I would be dead. I guess he thought I should have been grateful that he was even able to walk away. This guy did not have any visible marks on him, but I was about to put one on him. He is going to pay for this car one way or another, so I took him to court and the judge ordered him to pay me $4,000 because the car was totaled.

Mama's Boy

After bathing, feeding, and putting the kids to bed, we spoke most of the night. I know what you're thinking, and you could just stop thinking that. Yes, he stayed the night. Yes, he did sleep in my bed, and no, we didn't, and to make sure, I SLEPT IN SWEAT PANTS. We discussed several things. One thing that came out of this was honesty. He told me that he was sorry for the beginning of our relationship. He also admitted that he didn't love me enough. He said that he didn't know how to love, or knew what love felt like at least the kind that keeps on giving, and that's what I did I kept on giving but never got back. You know I wasn't upset at all, rather I was grateful. More than that I was grateful, that I was honest, honest with myself. Although I wasn't the same person he knew before he left, I grew up. I had a purpose. Along with that, I had Truth, Justice, and Wise.

Things were going fine, my children were going to school, he was driving me to and from school, and he even waited outside in the Volvo. That was my baby, the Volvo. I even named her Betsy. If you knew her, you would love her too. Everyone loved Betsy, everyone except Tango. Betsy always rained on his parade. What I mean is Betsy had a sunroof that leaked, so we carried an umbrella with us, and whoever was riding shotgun had to hold the umbrella up through the sunroof so we would not get wet. The funny thing was Betsy only worked for him. He would drive me to school for my Spanish class, and if anyone has ever taken a Spanish course in college, then you would know it was a two-hour course. I'm not sure what he was doing for those two hours, but I could see him under the hood of the car. My mom always told me, "Once you let a man fix your car, he could keep it running." Only thing is that it would only run for him.

I wonder how she knew where I lived. Oh yeah, I forgot, his mother came to my house uninvited, but this time she came with her cousin, but he wasn't here, and I don't think she believed me. Later that day his mother called, and I told her that he was not there. She said that he left his girlfriend's house yesterday to spend Mother's Day with her. I told her again that he was not here with me. She could have sworn he was here with me, and she was right. He was here, but he wasn't with me, right now. So I told her that I will have him call her when and if he comes back, but she insisted on calling back. Not a problem at first, but fifteen minutes later, she called again. This time my mother answered the phone and told her that he wasn't here. Again about fifteen minutes later, she called, this time I spoke with her and told her that as soon as he comes in, I will make sure he calls her and asked her, "Please don't call here again."

I just had to remind her that she told me not to call her home anymore, and that was just before his father passed away four years ago, and I respected her for that, but was it wrong to have asked her to respect me and not call my house anymore? I guess it was she told me that was her son, and that she was a sick woman, and that I shouldn't stop him from using the phone to call his mother. Well, he is the father of my children and will always be the father of my children, and when he does come in, I will give him twenty-five cents, and he can go out and call you.

I guess the honeymoon is over. He came in that night after hanging with my brother Tango. I told him his mother called and he should give her a call right away. He asked me why, what happened. I told him I have always respected his mother and she should respect the fact that someone other than her can love her son. He called his mother, and they got into a huge argument. I could hear her say she was going to tell his uncles on him. I couldn't believe it, I was defending her. I told him he should not be talking to her that way. He hung the phone up on her, or either she hung up on him. Either way we got into an argument that night over the way he spoke to his mother. I thought he was wrong not for calling her and apologizing, but for the way he spoke to her and the things that was said. Well, I guess he put me in my place. He said that was his mother and to let him handle his mother his way, so I never said another word about his mother, at least to him. I spoke to my mother about this situation, and she indicated that there are times when a man has to deal with things on their own, and in their own way. She also reminded me of the bond between a mother and her son, a bond that can and will not be broken. I respect that, but she should respect the fact that there is someone else in his life, and he needs to talk to her, but what could I say, he isn't talking to me at all.

Three nights of sleeping in the same bed and no, well, you know. Believe it or not, it was like this for three days. Until the knock on my bedroom door, it was my mother, she was telling us his cousin was on the phone, saying his mother had died. All I could do is sit there. He sat up on the side of the bed, and I sat with my mouth opened, as stiff as a board. I called his name several times, and he didn't answer. He stood up and got dressed as if he was in a trance, so I yelled down the basement steps for Tango to ride with us, only I couldn't start the car. He told me to get out and let him drive. Talking to myself, I thought, *He should not be driving.* But I didn't say a word. I thought we could get there and back without incident. We arrived at the house, and several people were standing outside. He got out of the car and told me he would be right back, so Tango and I sat there. Minutes later, he came to the car and told me to go home and that he would meet me there. I guess the people standing outside the house was his family. I just know this is a trick and that his mother called his family for support. I guess she told them about the conversation they had, but to call my house in the middle of the night and to come up with this story was childish. I thought they could have thought of something better than that. This was cruel. Well, it worked because he was staying, and I was headed home. He whispered something to Tango and walked away, so I guess that was it. He didn't want to speak to me anymore, and he wanted Tango to tell me it was over.

When I got home, my mother asked how he was doing. I told her I did not know because he wasn't speaking to me. My mom said, "Maybe this is his way of dealing with his mother's death." I'm sorry but I had to call the precinct to find out what was happening. Believe it or not, I did not believe she was dead. Believe it or not, I truly wished she was alive, so I could yell at them both for putting everyone through this. He did need to talk to his mother. I was thinking whatever his family has to say to him, I hope that it gets through to him and his mother, then we could move on. The operator on the phone asked me if I was calling about the death of the woman located at the address I had given them. I swallowed and said yes. They said the body was still in the house and the coroner hadn't been there to examine the body, so they didn't removed her yet. I was in shock, and it was my fault. They said she died of a heart attack and was found sitting at the kitchen table in her gown.

Two days had gone by now, and I hadn't heard from him. I called his mother's number over and over for two days and got no answer. I couldn't eat, I had migraines, and I took a leave of absence from school, but I continued to take the kids to school. His house was on the way to their school, so I stopped by to see if he was okay. Well, I guess he was, the house was a mess, and he looks as if he was drinking, which was understandable, but what I didn't understand was the condition of the bed, his mother's bed. It looks as though he had company. I didn't come there to argue with him, but this was no excuse. You know, it's time for me to go. There is mail all over the house, empty containers of food, the house is out of order, and he was in no condition to talk, so I decided to leave, but he asked me to stay, and I did. At first I couldn't understand a thing he was saying, and the more he talked, the more it didn't make sense. There was another woman here, and I bet I know who she was, that old chick from the Staten Island. I mean she was at least in her fifties. I remember he told me that his mother would have preferred her for him because she would have taken care of him, and there was nothing I could do for him except have babies. Did she ever think that maybe he wanted children or maybe we wanted to start a family? Okay, maybe I wanted to start my own family, but they are our kids, not hers. I can't believe it even in her death I am still having words with her, but that is what we did have words. Okay, not exactly to each other but the thoughts were there.

I asked him was someone else here in the house or in that bed with him. He just looked at me, and that was enough for me. I knew what that look meant. If there was anything I learned from my brothers, it was when they were doing something or someone, and he was doing both. As I headed for the door, he told me she was only here to help him make the arrangements for his mother's funeral. I thought he would have come to me for help, but I guess he didn't want my help nor did he want me. The funeral was in a few days, and he said he would like for us to be there. He also said he would call me later. I knew he had some of his mother's papers to go through, so I left and walked home. This gave me a chance to think. I knew this was over, and I was beginning to be okay with it. Who am I kidding? I wasn't okay, his mother is dead.

We met him at the house and took a cab to Brooklyn. There he was greeted by the rest of his family. I thought to myself, *Who is going to be the first to say something out of the way or insulting to me or my children.* Surprisingly, no one said anything. He didn't even say anything. He acted like we weren't even there. When the limo arrived, his cousin told me that we would ride in her car with her, behind the limo. You would have thought he would have told me himself, but I guess he was in that same mood, or either his family told him where everyone should ride. I guess it made sense because he had some relatives that were of grand age and should ride in the first car. What's wrong with me? He just buried his mother.

Okay, I didn't know anyone here, and I was expecting something to be said, but his cousin was nice. She talked to me and my children on the drive there and the drive back to the church. I really like her. She seems to know him very well, and he seemed to respect her. This is the cousin he would talk about whenever he spoke of his family. She was the one I could call whenever there was a problem. I felt comfortable with her, and she made me feel comfortable at the funeral. We made it back to the church, and it was getting late, so we took a cab back to Queens. He went back to his mother's house, and we went back to my house. It was a long day, so I gave the kids their bath, they ate their dinner, and they went to bed.

Another two weeks had passed, and I hadn't heard from him. I went back to school and continued to drop the kids off at their school. Only this time, I didn't stop by the house. I would walk past without even looking at the house. Okay, I looked, but quickly, and I kept on walking. One day as I was walking past, he asked me if we could talk. We talked for about an hour until I had to leave for school. At this point I didn't know what to say to him. He told me that he didn't have a family anymore and that his parents were dead. He even insisted that I didn't want to be with him. I told him that I didn't know where he got that from and that he did have a family. It's just that I don't think he's ready to be the head of this family. As I started to leave, he handed me a piece of paper stating he was three months behind in the rent. I asked him what was he going to do. He said he didn't know because he didn't have the money. I asked him if he would be here later. He said yeah. He was trying to clean up the house and make some phone calls. I told him I would stop by before I pick the kids up from school and we could see what could be done.

Well, he did clean up, and everything seems to be in the right place, that's if you call the kitchen table in the living room and bedroom pillows pushed against the wall with mounds of trash and mail piled on top of each pillow. Okay, let me see the letter you showed me earlier. Yep, he was three months behind, and final notice was stamped on it. I asked him if he had any luck with the bank. He said no. I told him I would stop by in the morning to call the bank and see if anything could be done to save his mother's house. He gave me this look as if to say thank you, but what came out of his mouth was "How were the kids?" I told him they were just fine. He said that he would call them later. No, not that he would see them later just that he would call them later. I guess he thought I was going to ask him when was he coming home, but I knew he needed to do this by himself, and to tell you the truth, maybe he need this time to reevaluate his life and see what his next move will be. At this point if he wants to be with that old chick, then let him. I wish him all the luck in the world. Besides, the kids haven't asked for him, and I didn't mention him. I guess by now they were getting used to not seeing him on a regular basis.

Going Postal

Wait, what am I doing this for? I have my own house and my own bills. Okay, stop. My mom always told me, "You don't hit someone when they are down because you never know when you are going to need that same someone." I took the kids to school and walked back to his house. He must have been thinking this morning because he was waiting at the front door, and he seemed to be sober because he uttered the words *good morning*. To tell you the truth, I didn't know if he was talking to me or talking to the tenants upstairs. As they were coming downstairs, I was walking past the house, and you could see them from the sidewalk. He tried to play it off by saying they were just checking the mail. I say they were just being nosey because I saw them check the mailbox when I was coming down the block. He must have said something to them about me because they didn't seem to be too happy to see me. Who did they think they were fooling at eight o'clock in the morning? Everyone knows that the mailmen didn't come to black neighborhoods until three o'clock. At least in my neighborhood, he always did.

I remember when my brothers and I were coming home from PS 95 (the PS stands for Public School number 95), we would race all the way up the street, and the last one home was a rotten egg. Well, you see I was always the rotten egg because I was too fat to keep up, so I walked back, but on the way back, I would see the mailman coming out of our neighbor's house. She would always wave at us kids, and I would always skip home, telling my mother, "I . . . see . . . the . . . mailman." My mom always knew it was time for the mail because he would go into her house when *Days of Our Lives* would come on and would deliver the mail when her son came home, which was the same time we came home because he went to school with us. I always wondered where her son got those sample packs of candy from, now I know. It wasn't that his mother worked in a candy store, it was that his mother got them from the mailman, and they were the samples that the neighbors were supposed to get in the mail.

Well, I called the bank, and they told me that they needed one thousand dollars because the mortgage payments were late. I asked him did he have any money. He said no. I told him that I didn't mean anything by this, but maybe his mother had some money hidden somewhere in the house. Sometimes grand people have a habit of having money tucked away in a sock, behind a picture, or under the mattress. He said he checked, and there was nothing. I asked him, "What about the tenants upstairs, didn't they pay rent?" He said that his mother had an arrangement with them, so I asked him what kind of an arrangement. He told me that they would pay $282 a month, as long as they run errands for her. Come on now, a two-bedroom apartment and an attic that rented for $280 a month. I couldn't believe it, so I rang the doorbell for the tenants upstairs to come downstairs so we could talk about the rent, but they were not home, so I called the bank back and told them they would have the money in the morning. The next day I stopped by and gave him $1,020 to send the money quick collect. From time to time, I would stop by the house to see if everything was okay, and all he would say was that he had some business to take care of and he would see me later. Well, that was my cue to leave. Obviously, he had been drinking. His skin was dark, and he looked as if he just got in, so I left.

One week later I got a call from the bank stating the mortgage was late, and if they didn't receive a payment of one thousand dollars, they would start foreclosure. I had a fit. What were they talking about? First of all, my mortgage is fifteen hundred dollars a month, and I just wired them the money. "Excuse me, sir," the woman said, "we only received part of the money, and we made arrangements for you to wire us one thousand dollars." That's when it clicked. He used part of the money to get something to drink, and the woman on the phone was from his bank and not mine. First of all, I'm not a sir, I am a miss, but my voice would fool anyone, and it usually did, especially those bill collectors. This time I'm not calling him, I called a cab and went to his house. Oh yeah, he was there, and he had the nerve to ask me what's wrong, Oh please. What did he think was wrong? I asked him why he didn't pay the whole thing. Of course he said, "What whole thing?" I may as well have been talking to myself. Okay, I'm going to take a shot in the dark with this one. "Did you get a letter from the bank or a phone call from the bank?"

"Well, not a phone call because the phone is disconnected now, and the place is a mess again."

This guy could not be for real, I know he is going through a rough time, but if he doesn't pull it together, he's going to feel even worse when they foreclose on his mother's house.

As I was talking to him, I heard the tenants get into a car outside. They must have taken their shoes off to come down the steps because I didn't hear a sound nor did I hear the door close, or maybe I was talking too loud. Whatever! I left a note for the tenants regarding their lease and told him I would be back. I returned two days later and met with the tenants. They told me that they had given him two hundred dollars last week and eighty-two dollars two days ago. As for the other tenant, he hasn't been home for three weeks. I guess they thought that was going to be the end of the conversation because they turned around and walked toward their steps.

WRONG. I told them that the prior arrangements are null and void and I will be giving them notice of their new rent and lease should they decide to stay. I was about to ask him about the rent they paid him, but I saw a letter from the bank, so I read it. Of course he got upset because he knew he didn't pay the amount I gave him. Damn, he only gave the bank nine hundred dollars, and if they did not receive one hundred dollars, plus an additional one thousand dollars by the fifth, then they would have no other choice than to start the foreclosure on the house. This time I will wire them the money, but before I do that, we need to take care of something. First, we needed to go to probate court and take care of his mother's estate, since the tenants are refusing to pay the rent. It took a couple of days before they cleared the estate. Second, I paid the mortgage company eleven hundred dollars. Finally, we went back to his house and started going through current bills and the mail just to see who he owed and what arrangements could be made. It was getting late, I was upset at him for letting this get so far so I left to pick up the kids, and to my surprise, he said thank you.

Leave Jack Out of It

He called me while I was in class and told me he was at the bank because he found his mother's bankbook and wanted to see if the account was closed. I guess it wasn't closed because he came to my house late that night and, of course, he had been drinking. He told me that his mother had money in her account and he was going to pay the bills. Come on now, who does he think he was talking to? This man is feeling no pain, and I'm not in the mood for this tonight. I just put the kids to bed, and I am in the middle of studying for my midterms, so good night. He could either sleep in the living room or go hangout in the basement with Tango and his friends. They were making so much noise down there I could barely study, let alone practice these Spanish words: *habla, hablamos, ha,* whatever. I passed the class, but not with flying colors. I earned a C.

The next morning I spoke to him about transferring the mortgage into his name and paying me back my money. He gave me three hundred dollars and told me to buy the kids something. He also said he would be back after he took care of some bills. Well, you and I both know what that was supposed to mean. It means that I would not see him for a month of Sundays and his money would be gone before the morning. So I told him that the bank called and needed to see him, or they may call in the loan. You know I was lying. I just wanted to get the money from him before he blows it on his friend Jack (Jack Daniels). I asked him if the bank asked for a secured amount to cover the next couple of months would he be able to pay it. He told me that he would and showed me an envelope of money. I told him that the bank usually ask for at least three months in advance, so he gave me three thousand dollars to hold for him and he left. I knew he was going to return not feeling any pain and wanting his money back along with some sorry story that he needed the money to pay the bills. Now who in the hell does he think he is fooling! Does he honestly believe I am buying his story that he is going to pay his bills this late in the night! I had to think fast before he came back. So the next morning, I called the bank and sent them a copy of the papers from probate court letting them know that the house was going to be turned over to him because he was the only child. I also asked if they would accept payments in advance with my signature on it. I guess they didn't care who signed as long as they were getting their money.

I should have taken the money he owed me out of what he had just given me to hold for him. If I do that, he will not be able to make the payments. This guy has no idea what he is in for, dealing with a house and tenants who are taking advantage of him. After all, he needs every dime he could get his hands on, besides I love him, he just doesn't know it. Of course, he returned and asked for the money, and of course, he was upset because I spent the money. He thought I spent the money on myself, and yeah, I let him have it, and I let him think that I took back the money that I had given him. I guess that really angered him. He left and I hadn't heard from him in three weeks, and three weeks later, he received a letter from the bank thanking him for the advanced payments. Since the mortgage payments were only three hundred thirty-three dollars a month, I figured since he had the money, he might as well make some payments. I don't know what was going on before, but from what I understand, those payments were behind from the time his mother passed until now. He was making the payments off and on, and never the whole payment. The bank continued to receive wired payments just so he could catch up with his mortgage.

I was in the basement washing clothes when I heard him ask my mother was I home. He came downstairs asking me what I was doing. Come on now, clothes in one hand, dry sheets in the other, and a bottle of bleach under my arm pits, what did he think I was doing? Before he could get the words out, I said to him, "Hard to apologize, huh." He just looked at me. I told him I received the same letter he had received, if that's why he stopped by my house. Yep, that's why he was here, to let me know that the bank got the payments. He knew deep down inside that I didn't take his money. He just needed someone to blame, but he couldn't blame me because I didn't do anything. He looked at me, and I looked at him. Okay, enough of this. I took the clean clothes upstairs, and I guess he was trying to figure me out.

The kids were outside playing, and Tango had just come from the car lot. He said he needed to get some sleep because he was doing the overnight shift since they fired the night watchman. His boss told him that they were robbed last night. When he saw Tango, he seemed to be relieved. They were partners in crime. I say that to say this, they would sit in the yard and smoke cigarettes, drink beer, and burn food on the grill. Yes, they would whistle at girls, at least Tango would, because when he tried, Tango would say here I come, or if I was sitting out there with them, Tango would call my name and say look at him he's looking at women as they walked by. Jokingly I would say something to him like, "Look at another women and your sleeping on the sofa." Or I would act like I was upset. In all honestly, men look at women. Shoot, they're human, they're not dead. He and Tango would sit in the yard eating, drinking, laughing, and joking with people as they walked past. Most of the people walking past they knew, or acted like they did, so they would invite them into the yard for some laughter and drinks.

Are You Kidding Me

For a while things seemed to be getting back to normal, but what is normal when you lose your mother. At first he was going past the house and collecting the rent, he said he had not heard from the tenant living in the attic, nor had he started cleaning his mother's house. He told me that he would get around to it next week. Well, next week came, and I had not seen him. He wasn't at the house or on the boulevard, and the tenants said the last time they saw him was when they gave him the rent. To tell you the truth, they were happy seeing him like that. This way they only gave him part of the rent and helped him drink up the rest. He was behind in the rent again, and I do believe they were trying to get him drunk enough to either lose the house or sign it over to them. Well, that was not about to happen.

I went home and called Tango. He went to visit his children who were living in Yonkers with their mother. As far as I know, Tango has three children, two by this girl in Yonkers and one that was living with me. But to hear him tell it, he has ten children. You heard that saying, "A ready-made family." Well, I hope he's ready to get another job because these girls already had children.

If he were to listen to anyone, he would listen to Tango because they were the best of friends. Tango came to Queens the next morning, and we drove to his mother's house. There we found him just sitting outside on the stoop. The front door was open, and it was dark inside even though it was about nine o'clock in the morning. Tango talked to him as they walked to the side of the house, as I stood in the front yard. I saw this man that I had not seen before come from upstairs. He introduced himself to me as the tenant who lived in the attic. He told me that he was just there to get the remainder of his things and that he was moving out.

They came from the side of the house as I approached the stoop. He said that he needed to get some things out of the house. He started looking around and said that he did not know where to start. Tango told him to just take his time. He walked to his mother's bedroom and turned the TV on. He then pushed the button, reached to the back of it, and unplugged it. Tango held the door as he carried the TV out to the car. When he returned, he opened up the shades and walked to the bedroom with his head down. Tango and I asked him if he needed any help, and he said no, so we told him that we would wait in the car. We waited about a half an hour before he came out and locked the door. Riding back to the house, he said he would come back tomorrow. He seemed really stressed. He and Tango were talking in the front of the car. He asked Tango if he was going back to Yonkers tonight. Tango told him that if he needed him, he would stick around. They drove me to school and hung out on campus. By the time I came out of my class, Tango had three or four girls' phone numbers. When I looked at him, he just put his hands up as if to say I had nothing to do with it. We all started to laugh. To tell you the truth, that is the first time we had a laugh in a while, which was what we all needed.

We stayed up pretty late that night, eating White Castle hamburgers and talking. We decided to go to his mother's house and help him clean up the next day. My mom said she would keep the kids while we were there cleaning, and since it was a Saturday, we were going to barbeque and have some friends over when we get back. I figured he has been through a lot lately, and he needs to see that there are people who loves him and cares about him. We started walking through the house when he noticed that some of his mother's things were missing. Some of her jewelry, her church hats, and even some of his father's things were missing. Tango went down the basement, and I went into the kitchen. He stayed in his mother's bedroom cleaning up. I boxed up some pots, pans, and dishes, and Tango cleaned the basement. Tango said he didn't throw away any important papers because he didn't know what he wanted and what he didn't want.

We packed and cleaned for nearly four hours. I told them let's call it quits for the day because I needed to get back to the kids and prepare for the barbeque. I carried some of the boxes from the kitchen to the car, and Tango was securing the basement door and taking out the trash from the basement. He was still in his mother's bedroom sorting through papers when he heard a movement from the upstairs tenants. It looks as if they were in a hurry. I heard the man tell the woman to come on, and she kept telling him to wait a minute. The next minute you know, they were all standing on the stoop talking. At first it seemed pretty friendly, then I heard them yelling at one another. Tango came from the back of the house asking what was going on. She told him to mind his own business. She told him that this doesn't concern him. Okay, that was it. I have seen and heard enough, so I walked across the street and approached her and asked her what was her problem. I also told her that she was not to talk to my brother like that. She started getting real nasty with everyone, and all he wanted to know is if they saw anyone going in and out of his mother's house. He also wanted to collect the rent they owed for this month.

I couldn't believe what I was hearing. This guy had the nerve to tell him that they did not owe him any rent since his mother was dead. They also told him that they made an arrangement with his mother that if anything ever happened to her that they could live there rent-free. Of course she backed him up with that ridiculous story, so I told her that they must be kidding. I also told them that they were going to pay the rent or they would have to find another place to live. He called me the B name and spit on him, so he grabbed him. She then turned and started to yell at me, which caused us to argue back and forth until Tango separated us. Before you knew it, he punched Tango in the back of the head and spit in his face. That's when Tango punched him in the face. The crazy thing about it was that he stopped Tango from hitting this guy again. The whole thing was unbelievable. The police came and arrested him and Tango. She even had the nerve to try and get me arrested. She told the police that I hit her. Believe me, I wanted to hit her, and I told the police if I hit her, she would definitely know it. I went to the house and told my mother what had happened and asked her if she could watch the kids a little while longer because I needed to go to the 113th precinct. By the time I arrived, they had already transported them to central bookings.

Well, it's Monday morning, and I needed to find them a lawyer. Because it was Friday they had to stay the weekend besides they both had a prior offense, and they were each given a bail. Do you know that fool went to the hospital and claimed he had a broken jaw. I doubt if it happened from the punch that Tango gave him. From what I heard, this guy was at the bar, got drunk, and got his a—whipped. I guess he took this opportunity to say he and Tango broke his jaw when they got into that argument in front of the house. I had to figure something out and quick. They needed someone to represent them, and I needed some money. Most of the lawyers I contacted wanted a five-thousand-dollar retainer fee, so I better seek an attorney. You see the difference between a lawyer and an attorney is that a lawyer usually handles lawsuits for clients or advises them of their legal rights and obligations in other situations, while an attorney is a legal agent who is qualified to act for people in legal matters. Well, I got them an attorney, and he was pretty good and he only charged a two-thousand dollar retainer fee. Not to mention he wasn't bad eye candy, the only problem with that was that he knew it, and so did his female colleagues. I noticed them noticing him and some of the males too. I mean, they were noticing his style. He often looked as if he just walked out of a *GQ* magazine. Did I mention he was like family? So it was hands off.

Surprisingly, it's not that crowded in here, especially being that it is a Monday morning. I met the attorney at the courthouse and discussed their case as the bus transported them from Rikers Island. They looked okay, just tired as they walked in with shackles on their feet and handcuffs around their wrist. I looked over at the defendants as they smiled. I thought, *If ever I needed a miracle, I needed it now.* The judge decided to postpone the case due to a murder trial, so they went back to Rikers, and I went home. When I arrived home, I received a call from Tango telling me they separated them and that he needed to speak with the attorney. I told them that he will be up there to see them as soon as possible and I will be up there to visit them as soon as I get the first floor apartment rented because we needed the money to pay their attorney.

My boys were home from karate school and could not wait to show off their karate moves in the yard, so we decided to barbeque in the backyard. It was easier, faster, and the best way to keep an eye on them. My aunts home attendant had been there all day. She even gave my aunt a bath and sat her in the lawn chair to relax before she ate her dinner. The kids were fed, they ate and ran around until they tired me out, so I called it a night and put them to bed. My mother and I tried to figure out how I was going to get the rest of the money to pay the attorney. He gave me a good price, but decisions had to be made. First, we decided to refinance the homes a couple of days ago, so we needed to add their names to the deed. This was so we could make the necessary home improvements and pay off some bills. The problem was that now they could possibly lose both homes—the one he grew up in and the one we grew up in. So I decided to speak with a lawyer in regards to a possible lawsuit. I found out that if the defendant won, he would be able to file a civil case against the both of them. Well, of course I was not about to let that happen so I thought fast. I had to explain to them when they called what was about to happen, and we all agreed not to transfer his mother's house into his name and not to add Tango's name on the deed. This way they could file a claim but would get nothing.

Well, the attorney called and said that we were on for court today. I thought I would at least get a day's noticed, but noooo. If I were going to court, then I would need to be there today. What am I complaining about? These guys have been in jail for three weeks, but it seems like forever. Classes are over this semester, so I don't have to worry about that, and I'm glad the kids are still in school, at least for the next month, and my nephew heard from his dad, Melo. If only he could have seen the look on this kid's face when he found out that his father was on the phone for him. He acts as if he won the lotto, and to him, his dad was the lotto. He hadn't seen his father in months, and for him to call him and tell him that he was coming by the house to see him, he was happy. Well, I rented the first floor apartment of his mother's house to a friend of the family. She was able to give me one month rent and one month security deposit. To my surprise she also wanted to purchase his mother's bedroom set and every piece of furniture in the place. It was hard to do, but we needed the money. I was able to pay the attorney and make arrangements to pay off the balance. So I met the attorney at his office to give him the payment, and I asked him, "How does the case look for these guys?" He said, "They will be fine." I trusted him, and he better be right.

I wanted to give the home attendant a two-week vacation, but with this court issue, I needed to play it by ear, besides I needed her help. I thought my other aunts would come by the house to give me a hand with her, but they didn't show up. In the beginning when my aunt first came to live with us, everyone told me that if I took care of her in my home, then they would come by to visit and help me out. They knew I had kids, they knew I was in school, and they knew I had my mother and two mortgages to deal with, but do you think they showed up; no, but that was okay. Tango was here to help me and so was he. At least they were here for me before they got arrested. So now I have to come up with the money to bail them out, that's if the judge is even going to set a bail. Two thousand dollars for him and five thousand dollars for Tango, the judge ordered. Now where in the world am I going to come up with the rest of the money, especially before their court hearing? A few days later, the attorney told me not to worry, so we returned to court, and he did his thing. First, he was released with time served, but Tango had to serve thirty days. I still wanted him out, but he said he could do the time. Besides the judge held Tango responsible for this idiot's broken jaw, when in reality he got into some kind of trouble being drunk and disorderly. He did have a broken jaw, but from who? All I know is that this guy had it coming.

We were on our way to Queens Bridge to pick up Tango, and just before we left, we heard that this was a bad neighborhood and that someone got shot and killed just the night before. We waited about two hours, and no Tango. Maybe he got a ride home from here, so we called the house, and my mother said that he was not going to be released tonight, so we headed home. We went back and forth like this for two days. One time Tango said a correction officer (CO) told him that he was going to make sure that he missed the bus, and he did. He missed the bus that night and had to wait until the next day because there were no other buses going out that night, and the CO put Tango on the schedule for the next night out. You see Tango liked joking and laughing with the other inmates. He failed to realize that he was the one that was scheduled to be released, but it didn't happen that night. Tango also told us that he got into it with one of the other inmates who knew Tango was going home, so he decided to pull a prank on Tango, because Tango knew about a prank that was pulled on that inmate and Tango said nothing about what was going to happen to him once he returned from lunch. When Tango returned to his cell, they wet him with buckets of water. He was soaked from head to toe, and he knew if he got mad or even with any of them, it would prolong his stay, and that's not what they wanted him to do. They really liked Tango, and they didn't want him to leave. To tell you the truth, he liked them to, but he wanted to go home, and I wanted him home.

"Ha ha ha ha ha ha ha, is that him?"

"Nah, it couldn't be him with those tight light blue sweat pants that only reached to the top of his high top skips, not to mention that busted-up T-shirt."

"Hey, Tango," he yelled, "Tango, hey, T dawg, over here."

He was moving real fast. I don't know if it's because he was cold or if he had a wedgy. Well, it was neither. He didn't want anyone to see him looking like that. I guess that's why he told him to stop calling out his name and just drive.

"Honestly, Tango, I didn't think they made those any more."

"Made what?" Tango asked. The spandex in magenta blue, he looked ridiculous, and we better get him out of here before someone picks him up and think he's on call.

You would have thought everyone would be asleep by now, but here on this block, the night is just beginning. They dropped me off at the house, said hello to ma dukes and rolled out. About an hour later, they returned with some murder burgers, that's what we called White Castle burgers, especially if you ate them late at night. The only way to get rid of those pains in the stomach was to eat more burgers first thing in the morning, but you have to admit that they were good. Shoot, I'm craving some right now.

First Things First

No more karate school for the boys, and no more beauty pageants for my daughter, summer is finally over, and the kids are back in school. Now the fun really begins, at least for Tango. You see, Tango has this first day of school ritual. He would wake us up extra early and do that stupid dance with straws up his nose. It was that first day of school dance that made everyone upset. Tango would help us into the bathroom by holding the back of our pajamas up high giving us wedgies. He would put the toothpaste on the toothbrush, never mind if it wasn't yours. He would just tell you that he would get you another one by the time you come from school. Tango would then hand you a bowl of cereal as you were walking toward the front door. Next he would shove your book bag either under your armpits or pack it on your back. Though you have to admit it, it was kind of funny, especially when he would walk to the front gate dancing while you were walking down the block crying. The only thing I could think about was someday it would be my turn, but that day never happened. My sister and her children had already moved out of the house by the time I graduated from high school. Speaking of school, I have four semesters to go before I earn my Associate's Degree in Community Health Education. I only hope and pray that I can find a job after graduation.

Now he wants to talk to me! Can you believe it, especially after what he did? You want to know what he did. Well, I'm going tell you what he did. Last night after cooking, and giving the kids their bath, I began washing and ironing their clothes, and Tango put my aunt to bed. I decided to take a quick shower; it was quick because the bathroom tub leaked downstairs between the kitchen and the dining room so fast that I had to put buckets on the counter and floor to catch the water. Well, after the shower, I grabbed my studying snacks—a pint of butter pecan ice cream, cheese curls, and three liters of cola. I am almost set.

I just have to wait for Tango to put some water in the boiler, get some matches, and wait for the wick to dry under the boiler before he could light the pilot.

Meanwhile, the heaters are keeping the upstairs warm, and the oven and four pots of water are keeping the downstairs warm. So now I'm set, I was ready for this all nighter. Two hours had gone by, and I was on my second assignment. Tango came upstairs from the basement after he got the boiler started and decided to make himself three grilled cheese sandwiches, homemade french fries, and some Tang. As he headed back downstairs, I heard someone tapping at my bedroom window. It scared the bejesus out of me. Tango asked me if I knew who it was. No I didn't know who it was, but I had a feeling who it might be, but the better question was what the hell did this guy want at two o'clock in the morning, and where the hell was he? He called over three hours ago and said he was on his way home. I asked him to stop knocking on the window and calling my name. Believe it or not, he told me he would stop knocking if I answered the front door. Well, he had a point, but I had a point too. I wanted him to stop knocking, go away, and for heaven's sakes stop yelling out my name.

He was drunk, I mean fallen-down drunk, and I'm not lying. He started flipping the mailbox lid up and down, so it would make a loud sound—*bang bang bang*. I figured I better open the door and talk to him, but when he spoke to me, I could barely understand what he was saying. No, I take that back, he said something that I was clear about, he tried to play the brother game on me. You see, the brother game is what I saw my brothers do when they wanted to get out of trouble with their girlfriends. They would get mad at their girlfriends before their girlfriends could get mad at them, especially when it was their fault in the first place. I do have to hand it to him, he tried, but he should have known not to try it on me. After all, I learned from the best. Don't get me wrong, I do love him, but I question it, you would too if after studying all night, sitting in the cold, and taking a quick shower. This guy started complaining and then decided to make up a story that he heard that some guy was at my house talking to me and he heard things were getting pretty close between me and this other guy.

Before I could say anything, he punched a hole in the closet door. Don't get it twisted, he didn't try to hit me, nor did he miss, he knew exactly what he was doing, at least he thought he did. The next morning, he acted as if he didn't know where the hole in the door came from. Tango told him that he needed to get his act together. He also told him that he didn't like missing his favorite TV show, the Odd Couple, just to babysit his ass. Last night, Tango came running upstairs from the basement. He thought the tub had finally fallen through the ceiling. He was yelling, "What happened now!" He knew once he got to the top of the steps and saw him standing there, this was going to be a long night.

He took him downstairs and tried to sober him up, but it didn't work. The best thing that he could have done was to fall asleep, and he did. Tango came back upstairs and asked me what happened. I told him, "I honestly didn't know." One minute he was knocking at my bedroom window, then flipping the mailbox, then punching a hole in the closet door and accusing me of spending time with another man. Well, the "spending time with another man" part was right. I was with another man yesterday, and I was hugging him, but that was no excuse. He had no right to punch a hole in the door. The next morning he came from downstairs and began walking toward the bedroom, and I was walking out of the bedroom when someone knocked on the front door. You could see it was a man through the screen door, but he didn't know who he was, and I could see he was upset because this man called my name.

While I'm waiting for him to open the door, he's looking back at me as if to say who the hell is this. As a matter of fact, he did ask who was this. He asked me if this was the man that I was with yesterday. I guess there were some things he did remember from the night before. I thought I was walking to the door alone, but when I looked back, he was standing right there. Before I could say anything, this guy stood in front of me and asked the man at the door what did he want. "Was he serious? I told you I would be back," Self replied, and boy, did that piss him off. "What's with this guy?" Self stated. "Is this the man you were with yesterday," he asked.

"As a matter of fact, yes, he is. Would you like for me to introduce? Self, this is my children's father." Of course he got upset before I could finish my sentence. He instantly went from "forget that I put a hole in the door" mode to who is pushing up on my woman. He has got to be kidding. I broke out with, "This is my brother, Self. Don't you remember him?" He stood there looking absolutely numb.

"What's up, man?"

Damn that, what the hell was he thinking? Did he seriously believe I would bring another guy to my house when at anytime he could pop up and see us together? Besides, I have too many things going on in my life, and I don't have the time to train another man.

I guess he thought the best way for him to apologize was to ask me to marry him, and he was smart, he waited until I was finished with midterms. He tried everything he could to be the perfect partner. He started off by picking the kids up from school early, taking them to the park, and spending a lot of time with them, in between all of that he was looking for a job. But first things first, I still had finals to get through and a whole lot of thinking and planning. For instance, we both had to get a job, a stable job, and the house needed some repairs, besides we had to find suitable tenants for his mother's second floor apartment now that the tenants had moved out, and we painted the apartment. "I guess what I am saying is YES, I will marry you."

Beautiful midnight blue and satin gray were the colors at our engagement party, and to top it off, it was a beautiful summer day. The kids were having fun, my mother and aunts were enjoying themselves on the stoop, and grill master Tango was throwing down on the grill. Believe it or not, he had not had a drink in months, and several places had called him in for an interview. Everything seemed to be going well, the first floor tenant was paying the rent, and we found tenants to rent the second floor apartment, life was good.

Maybe I spoke too soon. My aunt's Alzheimer's started to get the best of her. She started walking out the back door, and when you asked her where she was going, she would say she was going home. The only problem was that she dressed herself this morning, and she was wearing those clothes. She had placed her pocketbook on her head, I guess she believed it was her hat. She had on a sundress except it wasn't hers it was mine. She put on her winter coat and boots. One thing I could say about my aunt was that she could dress her a-- off, but I couldn't let her go out like that, she was too much of a classy lady.

I was told that maybe it was time to place her in a nursing home. What did they have to say that for? There was no way I was going to do that. Did they forget she is our aunt? One of our mother's sisters and besides black families don't do things like that, we stay together, and we did, at least for another year before my aunt became too ill for me to care for her. It became too much for her home attendant to take care of her, and we just couldn't do it anymore. It was the hardest thing to do, I loved her so much. Now the task was to locate a good nursing home, which was hard to do especially after I heard stories of nursing homes not caring for the elderly, but this one did and it was close to home. As a matter of fact, it was in walking distance from the house, so someone was always able to visit her at the nursing home.

Back to the Drawing Board

Okay, my kids are growing up, and I am not getting any younger. Another year has gone by and another year of school, at least this is my last year. You would think he would be happy for me, for us. This degree, although it is an associate's degree, is an accomplishment, and I am not going to let anyone take this feeling from me. So here he is again with that whoa-is-me attitude and, of course, his excuse to drink, but you know what, buddy, you don't need an excuse to drink nor do you need an excuse to stay with me and the kids. No one is holding him here, nor is anyone expecting him to stand up and do the right thing that's even if he knew what the right thing was. I am not going through this again. I'm already a year behind due to the TIA, and now he wants to act a fool. Well, count me out, buddy, and no, thank you. So I let him stew in his own crap for weeks without letting him know that he was working on my last nerve. Okay, so they didn't give him the job, it doesn't mean that he should give up. Just go out there and look for another one, and another one and another one, until you get that job.

Either Jack is getting to him, or some of his friends are telling him something ridiculous, like go get the rent money from the tenants. Between the two homes and the money I received from the accident, we were barely making it, heaven forbid if something went wrong and we needed to make some repairs. Someone upstairs must be looking out for him because the toy store called him in for an interview, and it could not have come at a better time. It was just after Thanksgiving and most stores are doing their holiday hiring. They wanted him to come in for an interview on Tuesday at 9:00 a.m., so I took the message and could not wait for him to walk through the door to give him the good news, but he didn't come in that night, nor did he come in the next night, or the night after that. At this point I was done, done raising a grown man. That was a job his parents were supposed to do. Instead of giving him what he wanted, they should have given him what he needed, but they couldn't do that. They were too busy spoiling his a-- and trying to outdo the rest of his family, so what, they owned a home, and most of their family lived in apartments. Big deal, you were given the opportunity to raise this child into being a man, and they were failing him, they failed him so bad that he abused life.

They could have done a better job at raising him. As for his father, I believe it was pride and to make his wife happy by allowing her to raise a child because they never had a child of their own. At least that's what they wanted me to believe, but I heard it through the grapevine that they did have a daughter whom they did not raise, nor did they have any contact with. However, his mother I believe thought she could show the rest of her family that she could do something with him, and that she could do a better job than his natural mother which was actually her niece. So she could offer him a house, money, two parents, but what I believe she did was show him off at family gatherings. "See how clean and neat he is, watch how he sits up straight", but their house did not make it his home. As for showing him off, to me it was more like throwing it in someone's face, in other words it was bragging rights. But, but bragging rights to what they were all family and that's what I thought family do, take care of one another. You see there is a much bigger picture to his family than I was lead to believe, and all of the people who could have shed some light on his dysfunction were now deceased, and those family members who are still alive and could shed some light on his life blew the lights out on him a long time ago.

Looky, looky, he finally came home and looking wide-eyed as if I didn't know he was drinking. You would think he would want to talk to me, but instead he headed for the basement so he could speak with Tango, but this time Tango was not there. Tango went back to Yonkers for a couple of days, so it was back to the drawing board. Of course he tried the argument thing, but when he saw that wasn't going to work, he tried talking to my mother, but she wasn't there either. She was in the hospital for her asthma, so the only one left he could talk to and should talk to was me, but I didn't want to talk to him. I just gave him the information, closed the bedroom door, and went to sleep. The next morning he was showered, shaved, and shining. I didn't say a word to him. He got dressed while I fed the kids and took them to school. By the time I got home from school and picked up the kids, he was sitting in the living room talking to my mother who came home that morning after lying on a hospital gurney all night long.

I handed it to him, to both of them. To tell you the truth, they had jokes, they had the nerve to be looking at bridal magazines. His was turned to the tuxedo page, and hers was turned to the wedding gowns. I told him that he would look very handsome in a tux and my mother would make him a beautiful bride. As long as I had those books, he never once looked through it or showed any interest in picking out any tux, so at this point I was tired, tired of all the crap and tired of trying. He must have told him one hell of a story because Tango was home. He got paid so he ordered Chinese food for everyone, everyone except me. No, it's not that he didn't want to order me something to eat, it's that I'm allergic to Chinese food. As a matter of fact, I'm also allergic to seafood, all except tuna fish, go figure.

As the kids ate their food, I showered and got ready for bed. In all honesty I wanted him to get them ready for bed, and I do believe at this point he would have done anything I wanted him to because he knew I was not speaking to him, but instead I got the kids ready for bed. They asked me what I was going to eat for dinner, I told them I wasn't hungry, I was just tired, so Smokey started singing. At first I couldn't make out what he was singing, then I was trying to figure out why he was singing ain't that good news, but I soon found out when I saw his security badge from the toy store lying on the bed. He began talking a mile a minute, and all I could do was look at him with a blank face. I told him that was good news for him and I was happy for him for real, and if that's what he wanted, then that's good, but I was done, I was tired and at a loss.

Is It Me?

Graduation is next week. Can you believe it? And the decorations for my engagement party are midnight blue and silver. Yes, I said my engagement party. We talked about things and seemed to be working things out. He's still working and haven't had a drink in a while. Things are good, but they would be better if he was to attend an Alcoholics Anonymous meeting. The graduation was nice, although it was exhausting preparing for it. I couldn't enjoy it as much as I wish I could have because I wasn't feeling well, but by the time of the engagement party, I was feeling much better. The party lasted for two days. On top of that, Tango had the music blasting so loud that it could have been heard all the way to Peter's Field Park.

Now the hard part begins with the kids being a year older and wanting name brand jeans, sneakers, and jackets and me needing to find a job and going to school part-time. I know I needed a job, but I needed my bachelor's degree even more, so I decided to reenroll at York College. Believe it or not, this was the same school I was academically dismissed from, but that was my fault. I wasn't ready for school then, but I'm ready now. Thank you, Jeezus, I found a job. I began working as a substitute teacher at this private school, which was really cool, but I was tired most of the time especially with this part-time job, school, and the kids. Don't get me wrong, I appreciate everything God has done for me, not to mention keeping this man with a job. It was the planning of my wedding that was taking a toll on me, and something had to give, so I decided to leave this job and finish school. I thought with the money coming in from both homes and him working at the toy store, we would be just fine. But things weren't fine. Both homes needed repairs, and the tenants were always late with their rent. So I started the paperwork and evicted the upstairs tenant, painted the apartment over, and rented the apartment to someone who seemed a bit more stable. I was also able to rent out the basement, so that bought in a couple of more dollars.

I didn't attend school the next semester. Instead I took a leave of absence because I was offered a job as an intervention specialist at an HIV clinic. At first I thought all I have to do was pass out condoms and pamphlets, then I found out that I would actually have to engage in a conversation with women about protection, HIV, and AIDS. Well, I was no expert, but I did know how to protect myself. I remember the first day on the street with the condoms. It was at 40 projects. I was told 40 projects got its name from the 40 little projects in the neighborhood, but to this day I still don't know where the name came from, but it was a pretty cool neighborhood. Our first day on the streets, I traveled with three intervention specialist including myself, about five or six peer educators, two case managers, and our supervisor who looked scared to death. She decided to divide us up into two teams and meet at PS 40. After about two hours on the streets, I thought to myself, *I gave up college for this*. I mean all we did was walk around the community and talk to some of the women who were the population we were to focus on.

Maybe it was me, but when we got back to the office, we had a meeting about our first day in the community. Everyone gave their feedback, but you know me, I had a little more than feedback to give, I had an opinion. I wanted to know why we were giving information and condoms to women only when it takes two to infect. I mean, the men needed just as much protection as the women. This is not only a woman's infection—it infects, effects, and affects us all. Well, the answer I was given was that it was a grant-funded program and women were our target population. Okay, call me insubordinate, but the next day I hit the street, I was partnered with a real cool peer educator. She said she knew the streets, and she also told me that she lived in 40 projects, so we decided to put a little twist into our intervention. We would sit at a bench near other people, and we would talk loud about our job and condoms, especially the fact that we had flavored condoms: grape, banana, chocolate, and everyone's favorite cherry. We took out the condoms and handed them to each other. We laughed, tossed them back and forth, we opened them, and demonstrated with the condoms, shoot, we even talked about each other's boyfriends as if we knew them. It was funny, and it became a part of our routine, we could have gotten fired behind that but it got the job done, and the outcome was a success.

We quickly became known as the condom ladies. We gave condoms to men, women, and seniors. Yes, seniors, they asked and we gave. I remember back in the day when I was a kid, we called adults who used drugs junkies. Well, those adults are now these seniors, and they were in everyone's neighborhood. These are the seniors who are getting their Social Security checks on the first of the month, and by the third of the month, they are already broke. In some communities, seniors were preyed upon by young females who accompanied them when cashing their checks. They would then return to the apartment and have a good time drinking and sexing. I guess it was a give-and-take arrangement, but little did they know they were giving each other HIV and taking it home to their families. Don't get me wrong, the young males would do the same thing with the older women who seem to enjoy the company of a young male around their development. I don't think they were there just fixing the pipes. They supplied the cleaning solution (drugs, HIV, you name it), and I guess they had a good time because everyone knew everyone and that happened in most of the neighborhoods we walked through in Queens that had projects or apartment buildings.

There were times we would go out into the street and see young women no older than eighteen or nineteen years of age walking back and forth. Well, our job was to engage in conversation hoping that the conversation would convince them to come into the clinic. It was easier said than done. One day, this female was leaning in this car window talking to this guy and when she finished, we started talking to her. At first she didn't want to talk to us, but about ten minutes later, it was mission accomplished, but you know it felt more than a mission. It felt as though she was one of our daughters, or little sister. We knew she was prostituting and didn't want to take the condoms, so we passed it to her in a money envelope and told her to come see us at the clinic. To this day I wonder if she ever got herself off the street. It was a sad situation and the most dangerous situation I was ever in. What if her pimp had come along and saw her talking to us, what would he have done? Better question, what would we have done?

Could you imagine that being one of your daughters, nieces, or cousins? Well, that got me to thinking about my daughter and the birds and the bees. I didn't hesitate when it came to bring your daughter to work day. I decided to bring my daughter to work, but I don't think her teacher liked her discussing my job with the other students. Instead of my daughter telling her classmates that her mother counseled women, she decided to bring a condom to school for show and tell. Yes, I got a phone call from the principal, and we had a meeting about my daughter's show and tell. I explained it to the principal of how important it was for me to take my daughter to work with me, and at the same time explain to her another important part of life. To this day some people question my judgment of taking her to work with me. No, she didn't see any prostitutes, nor did she see us passing out any condoms, but what she did see was her mother hard at work and men and women in need of assistance. It was my decision, and I don't regret it for one bit except the part where she bought the condom to school. I mean that child wasted a good condom, and it was the cherry flavored one too.

Unbelievable

Everything is going to be so beautiful. It's two days before the wedding. The cake was finally ordered—the tent, table, and chairs will be delivered and set up the morning of the wedding. The bridesmaids' dresses are a beautiful champagne color, the groomsmen's tuxedos were picked up, and each man had the right shoes. The yard was beautifully decorated, and I had two bouquets of flowers, one was a keepsake and one was a throw-away bouquet. What I mean by a throw-away bouquet was that the bride will throw away a bouquet of flowers to all the single women at the wedding, and whoever catches the bouquet of flowers is supposed to be the next in line to get married and the other bouquet I will keep. I even had two wedding gowns. I bought one gown last year, and then I lost some weight, so I bought another gown, and I couldn't make up my mind. And yes, both gowns were ivory.

Okay, I must be getting punked, and I don't think this is the time to be playing games with me. The caterer called and told me that the order I placed for the wedding could not be filled and that he apologized, but he didn't give a reason. What in the hell was I supposed to do for food? Before I knew it, the company that was supposed to deliver the tent, table, and chairs cancelled. They said that they did not have the size tent I needed and they did not have enough tables and chairs. And if that wasn't enough, the woman who was making the cake called and told me that the color of the cake did not come out the way she had planned and she did not have enough time to make another one. I just wanted to scream, this cannot be happening, and where in the hell is he. He left hours ago to get a haircut, and it's not that far of a walk from the house to the barbershop on Farmers Boulevard.

Beauty was able to call in a favor to this church who cooked food for special occasions, so they were able to cater the food. I received the deposit back from the company I ordered the tent, table, and chairs from and found another place down Atlantic Avenue, which was able to fill my order, deliver, and set up the table, tent, and chairs just in time for the ceremony. I was also able to rent an arch so we could stand in front of it while the minister performed the ceremony. Everything seemed to be back on track. I even settled for the cake in another color, but what I could not settle for was a bridegroom that vanished, and no one seems to know where he was. He told Tango he was going to get his haircut, but the barber said he didn't see him.

It's the morning of the wedding, and still no bridegroom. My hair, makeup, and nails weren't done, and the boys needed their haircut as well. The farthest I got was my daughter's hair, and I hope it last until four o'clock. The yard was set up with the tables covered in gold and ivory, the tent covered the nearly one-hundred-foot yard. The good news was that my bridesmaids were to arrive at three, and the photographer called and said that he was going to arrive at one to take pictures of the bridal party as they were getting ready for the wedding. Everyone was accounted for except him. Even the calypso band arrived early to set up their equipment. Tango decided to relieve me of some of the pressure, so he took the boys to the barbershop to get a haircut, and I went to the beauty parlor to get my hair done. I just hope I have enough time to get to the nail shop on Hollis Avenue to get my nails done.

Beauty and I met up so I could give her the money to pay the church for the food they cooked. It was getting late, and no one heard a word from him, so I decided I may as well call off the wedding, but Beauty told me not to call off the wedding, just to turn this wedding into a party and call it a day. I started to call the bridesmaids and tell them to bring a change of clothes and comfortable shoes so we could party, but before I could make the first phone call, he took the phone from me and asked me was I ready, ready, ready for what? Is that all he has to say to me—am I ready? Maybe he should begin with where he was, and don't start with he was at a bachelor's party because I threw him a bachelor's party with Tango's help. Shoot, I even suggested getting them three strippers, so he better come up with something better than that, and he did. And boy, was it original. He said he needed time to think. "Dude, you're the one who proposed so what is there to think about?" To be honest I had to put myself in his shoes for a minute. This would be his third marriage, and I guess he doesn't want this one to fail like the rest of them.

Wait, why am I putting words in my head? The truth of the matter is, he knew his mother didn't like me, and he's probably wondering if he is making the mistake of his life, when he should be wondering if he was making the mistake of my life. Well, I had nothing to lose. He signed a prenuptial agreement, which also included the care of our children in the event of my death, both homes, any debt he had before the marriage, and any debt he would gain during the marriage would be his. I loved him, but did he love me enough? So I asked him if he loved me, and we said I do.

Now Wait a Minute

I kept my job as an intervention specialist for a couple of more months while I worked part-time as a life skills specialist in a group home. We really needed the money. He had lost his job, and Quick was living in the house with his girlfriend and her two kids. He also had his friend, the weasel, living in the basement. By this time, Tango's girlfriend had left and returned to her family in the south, and my nephew had stopped going to school. There was more traffic going in and out the side door than enough. I complained to my mother about it on several occasions, and I also got into several arguments with Quick about all the traffic, especially since it was his traffic. He had it all set up, and his friend, the little weasel, kept the door opening and closing all hours of the night. But what I could not understand was how were these guys, who did not have a job; be able to afford trips to Atlantic City, jewelry, new clothes, and little motorbikes for his girlfriend's kids. It doesn't take a rocket scientist to figure it out, so I decided to confront them about it, and of course, it turned into an argument between me, Quick, and the little weasel. I wanted them out of the house. I wanted what they were doing out of the house. It was ridiculous, and I couldn't believe it. They didn't care about nothing or no one.

My nephew wasn't the best student in the world, but he was still in high school, up until Quick decided he didn't need school. He began hanging with Quick, the weasel, and their friends. He would sleep all day and be up all night. He babysat each time they took a trip outside of New York. I couldn't believe it. They could get this boy up early in the morning so he could babysit, but they couldn't get him up so he could go to school. As long as they bought him a new pair of Tims, he was happy. He even started wearing his pants hanging off his little a--. Who would have ever thought this was the same little boy, I was raising, who was in in kindergarten going to school wearing a shirt, tie, a pair of penny loafers, and carrying an attaché case. He was really cute, he was my baby and they was making him a little man.

I really enjoyed working at the group home, but between the tenants giving me a hard time, Quick and his friends doing their thing in the basement, the constant arguments with them, and my kid's school calling me about my Truth's behavior. I had enough, so I called the police and informed them that I believed there was a lot of traffic in and out of my side door, and I do believe drugs were being sold from my home. Of course no one liked the idea that I called the police, but what else was I supposed to do, they didn't want to leave. I was tired of arguing, and I didn't want this around Truth, Justice, and Wise. I thought this should put an end to it all, but to my surprise, it didn't. That just made things worse. I was told that this was a family matter and that I would have to take this to family court. Wait a minute, did I hear the police right that this was a family matter and I should take this to family court. For a drug issue, was he serious? Well, I guess he was serious because they left without taking an incident report.

Things quieted down for a few days and rightfully so because no one was speaking to me. Of course, Quick was furious. He told his girlfriend not to speak to me, and her children were kept in the room. My mother seemed to be a little upset. Truthfully speaking, I don't know whether she was upset with me calling the police or if she was upset with the fact that this was happening in her house. Whatever the case, it had to stop. It was affecting my children, and I was not having it anymore. The first opportunity I got I was going to get out, but a part of me was saying why should we be the ones who leave after all I owned the house, at least part of it. My mother was the co-owner, so when the house next door to our rental property went up for sale, I decided to look into purchasing the home. I had some money saved up, but it wasn't enough, so I had to work overtime at the group home for a couple of months.

Of course, he began to drink again and do his famous disappearing act. As usual, I had to rely on Tango to watch our kids so I could work the overnight shift as a life skills specialist, and during the day as an intervention specialist. In order for me to work as a life skills specialist, I would slip away while I was in the field at three o'clock and not take a lunch on those days, so I could report to work at the group home until midnight, and in some cases I would work a double, which meant I would work until the next morning. The night shift had its moments. Sometimes, the girls would try and sneak out, and other times, they would fight, but it was all worth it to see my kids the next morning and watch Saturday morning cartoons with them.

I couldn't do any of this without Tango's help. He had them dressed, fed, and right in front of the TV when I arrived home. I know Tango had his own life, but he knew I wanted to get out of here, and he was my only hope. Tango would work the overnight shift at the car lot when I didn't work the overnight shift at the group home. Other than that, he would work during the day in the car lot, selling and cleaning cars. I think the best part of working at the car lot for Tango was when he took customers out for their test drive. There he got to meet a lot of women, and women were his thing.

A couple of months later, the group home opened up a home for teen mothers and infants right off Jamaica Avenue. That night some of the workers on the four-to-twelve shifts at the Dunkirk house told me about a new position within the agency, so I applied for the job. A week later I was called for an interview with the house manager and was later notified that I got the job. This was right up my alley, I could quit the job at the clinic, work some overtime, and in no time at all, I should be able to save up some money so I could purchase the other house.

Truth, Justice, and Wise seemed to enjoy their new beds. I was able to save up enough money to purchase a new bunk bed for Justice, you know the one that included a desk. I decided to buy her that one since she likes to write and draw. I figured this one would be perfect. I thought it would be better to get Truth and Wise beds with headboards that had several different compartments, since Truth liked to collect Power Rangers. It would be a good way for him to keep his collection off the floor, and Wise liked to collect cars and make little forts. My bank account was growing, but as fast as I was able to save the money, it was as fast as I was spending the money. I still had to pay the bills at each house, and I couldn't refinance any more there because there was little equity in both homes and he was coming and going without a job. Besides those repairs on both homes were costing me a lot of money, but the homes needed to be repaired.

It has been a month since I started at MIP four, the teen mother-infant group home. I knew this is where I needed and wanted to be. The girls were great, and the infants were beautiful. I gave all their babies nicknames like Rosa Parks, Mr. Jefferson, and Big Pun. These names really fit each one of these babies' personalities. Let's not forget about the staff. We had our good days, and we had our bad days, but most of all, we had a great supervisor.

She was really good to me and my family, especially during the time when my Truth went into the hospital. I was working the eight to four shift at this time. It was the perfect schedule. It allowed me to be at home with the kids and work some overtime during the four to twelve, if I needed it. Well, this one particular day, Truth's school called and said that he was having some problems in school and that I needed to come to the school. When I arrived at the school, they told me that they had taken him to the hospital because he threatened to harm himself and another student. They evaluated Truth after a couple of hours and then released him back to me. I had a meeting with his school principal, and we agreed that this placement was not the best place for him, so he was transferred to another school. This school was much smaller than his previous school, and the classroom setting was much different. The teacher ratio was greater, and they had a variety of activities for the students. I thought great, a better school and a better school year for Truth.

Things seemed to be heating up again around the house. This time they were standing on the front stoop and their people, or customers if that's what you want to call them, would walk back and forth whenever they wanted to make a purchase. The little weasel would see them and meet them on the side of the garage. They would walk up the alleyway, and he would lean across the fence and make his sale. He probably kept his stash in one of the trees. We had an apple tree, cherry tree, and a pear tree, take your pick. I knew he hid it somewhere. I wouldn't be too surprised if he didn't hide his stash somewhere near the grapevine we had in the backyard next to the barbecue pit.

The arguments started again, and the police was called again. It was the same thing over and over again until this one day when I asked my mother to watch the children until we come back from grocery shopping I had just got off from working the eight-to-four shift at MIP four, and I also worked some overtime at the transitional house for about two hours because they were short staff. The transitional house is for girls who reached the age of eighteen but are not quite ready to live on their own, so they remain in placement while they work, attend college, or finish high school. None of the girls in the home have babies or over the age of twenty one. However, they continue to need supervision.

The lines in the supermarket were very long, and it was getting late, so I called my mother and asked her if she had any money on her until I get home. This way she could order Chinese food for the kids and I could repay her when I got back home. She said she had the money and would call the order in to the restaurant. Finally, we reached the cash register, so I asked him to call a cab from around the way, which usually took forever to come. We arrived home about ten thirty, and we couldn't have gotten there any faster. I had to use the bathroom and felt as though I was going to explode. I'm glad it wasn't that time of the month because I would have exploded. You know holding that urine and . . . Well, you get the picture. I made it up the steps so fast that I didn't get a chance to pay the driver. All I know is that I grabbed four bags of grocery and made my way up the steps. I don't know how I did it, but I reached the top of the stoop in record time. I knocked on the door several times, but there was no answer, so I knocked again, still no answer. I didn't have a key, so I couldn't let myself in. To tell you the truth, no one ever really had a key to the house because someone was always home. As I dropped the bags and turned to knock on the front window, my ultimate nightmare was actually a reality. Someone dressed in all black had covered my mouth and grabbed me in the chest and told me to come in, sit down, and shut up. I was horrified. I saw my children lying on the floor faced down. My mother was sitting in a chair with her back to the window, and additional men were walking in and out of rooms and going up and down the stairs, including the basement.

What in the hell is going on? Who in the hell are these people? What do they want? All sorts of questions were going through my head. What are they after? Who do they want? The hallway door closed, then I heard the front door open and close. The next thing I noticed he was snatched into the hallway, thrown against the wall head first, and questioned as to who he was. At this point I was totally confused. What could they possibly want with him? After the questioning, they told him to come in, sit down, and not say a word. Okay, that was fine, but we still had grocery in the cab, and the cab driver was slowly approaching the steps with some of the grocery. I told them we had bags outside in the cab and we needed to get them before the cab driver started asking questions, but it was too late, he was already in the hallway with these guys, and he didn't look too happy. I was told that I could take one of the kids outside to get the rest of the bags, and I was told not to say anything to anyone if anyone approached the house.

I took Truth to the front door and told him to hold the screen door open while I throw him the bags. I also told him if a car approaches and someone starts to shoot, he was supposed to close the door and run in the house without looking back. As the cab driver handed me the bags, I saw an odd look on his face, but I couldn't figure out what it was. I didn't know whether he was afraid of what he was told or if he wanted to tell me he was going to call for help. I took it by the way he pulled off in his car that he was afraid of what he was told. Well, I had a few bags in my hands, and Truth was standing in the doorway. Before I could make a complete turn, a small red car pulled up and asked me if I knew how to get to Hollis Avenue. My instincts wanted to tell him to turn the car around, go all the way to the light, make a left, then a quick right, go about two blocks, and he would be at the intersection of Hollis Avenue and another street I was so confused that I forgot the name of the other street. You would think after living in this neighborhood for so many years I would have known the name of that other street. But I couldn't, Truth was standing in the front door, and when I looked up there were men on the balcony and on the side of the house. I didn't notice it the first time we pulled up to the house, but who approaches their home expecting their house to be surrounded by men in black.

I stood in the walkway of my front yard spread like the letter T. My arms were held out away from my body with two bags of grocery in each hand. I nodded no with my eyes shut and continued to walk toward the house. I just knew this was it. It was going to go down right here and right now. I told Truth to go back inside and close the door. I also told him that I was coming in right behind him. Once inside, I was told to place the bags on the floor. I don't know, maybe I didn't hear them because I kept walking into the dining room and I placed the bags on the table and put my head down. One of the gentlemen came into the dining room and decided to ask me if he could talk to me. At the same time, my kids were saying they had to use the bathroom and that they were sleepy. One of the men told them to wait, but the guy in the room with me told him to let the kids go to the bathroom and allow them to sit on the sofa. I walked him to my bedroom door, and he identified himself as an officer of the law, what part of the law I don't know. All I know is that I was beyond caring who they were, I just wanted this to be over one way or another.

He explained to me that my brother Quick was sitting in the front room with handcuffs on and that he was under arrest. He also told me that they would be arresting my nephew as well. He was sitting in the corner of the living room, near the closet, so I didn't see him when I came in the house the first time. He also told me that they were trying to get more information from Quick, and if he didn't give it to them, they would then remove my children. Well, now we have a problem because they were leaving this house with my children over my dead body. I asked them what information did they need, and if I could be of any assistance, I mean any assistance.

I would help them in any way as long as they left my kids alone. I asked them if I could see Quick for one minute, and they told me no. I couldn't see him or speak to him. I heard one of the men say on the walkie-talkie that a woman was approaching the house, so they brought me back into the living room and sat me down. We managed to sit next to one another, so he asked me what was going on, and I told him that I really didn't know. All I wanted to do was to make sure the kids and my mother were okay. A knock came to the front door, and a young pregnant girl appeared. They brought her into the hallway and asked her some questions.

The officer in the living room cracked open the door just enough so I could see her. He asked me if I knew her. I told him that I never saw her a day in my life. I asked him if I could talk to her. He said no and shut the door. From what I could tell, she was arrested and led out of the house, but before you knew it, another knock came to the door. This time they let the person walk in and spoke to her by using her name. "Hello, Coffee," they said. With my eyebrows raised, I looked at her, and she looked at me. They took her into the front room along with two officers and closed the door. About twenty minutes later, my nephew and Quick were being led out of the house in handcuffs, and Coffee left without saying a word. At this point I was no longer afraid. I was pissed off. "WHAT IN THE HELL IS GOING ON HERE, and where is the little weasel in all of this? Don't tell me he didn't get arrested too? Please, please, please don't tell me he got away?"

The officer that I had spoken to earlier walked me to the rear of the house and explained to me that Quick had given them enough information, so they would not be removing my children. They told me that they couldn't tell me anything else except the house was clear and my children could go to bed. As he was being led out of the house, Quick looked at my mom and told her that everything was going to be all right. At that point, I didn't care what happened to him or anyone else caught up in this mess. We put the kids to bed once they left the house in handcuffs and returned to the living room. I looked at my mother and noticed that she was pretty shaken up. She just kept looking down shaking her head. I asked her if she was okay or if she needed to go to the hospital? She replied no. I didn't want to ask her too many questions, so I told her I would call the ambulance and ride with her. Again she said no and that she would be okay once she used her nebulizer. She held it together pretty well even though she sat in that chair for hours.

I almost forgot that we didn't eat, but who could eat after all of this. I walked my mother upstairs and checked the kids one more time just to make sure they were asleep. I called their names several times, but they didn't answer. Either they were practicing what they were taught to do and that was to play dead or they were really asleep. I looked at him and he looked at me, we checked the rest of the house, and it was secured, at least secured enough for use to breathe. I know it may sound cruel, but all I could say was that it was over and maybe now my house could return to normal, but what is normal around here? With people coming and going, how do we get back to normal when we still don't know what normal is, or what will happen next?

My nephew came home the next morning looking as if he had been in jail for six years. He looked stunned, and he should be stunned. Did he think this was all a dream? He looked at me as if he wanted to cry, and I looked at him with disappointment, outrage, and sadness, but he was my baby too. I had him since he was five years old, and now he is sixteen years old, and he had a criminal record. Don't get me wrong, he is a good kid, he just got caught up with the wrong people. Unfortunately, the wrong people was family, the same people that is supposed to protect you, love you, and nurture you. I guess the way this family loves, nurture, and protect is to use, misuse, and abuse. I know all three first hand. I felt used for so many different reasons.

Maybe it's me, but I thought if one mother could love and take care of eight children, then eight children can certainly love and take care of one mother. Come to think of it, as long as I was home and took care of my mother, nieces and nephews, and the house, then that left it open for my brothers and sister to enjoy the rest of their lives. After all I didn't have a life of my own, heaven forbid it if I began to live. What was I thinking? I should have left the first chance I got, but I couldn't, that was my mother, and who was going to take care of those kids? I didn't want them to go through what I went through, no one having your back and dealing with this family alone. This was one house that was not a home. Well, maybe to them it was a home, and they knew there always had a place to stay when they couldn't make it on their own. Someone would always come back here, and some came with baggage, girlfriends, babies, and friends.

Although he was no longer living, his spirit was very much alive, and I felt as though he always had a hold on me. I couldn't tell anyone what he did. I thought he was going to hurt my mother. He was a different kind of man. He was a man of sorts. Besides, I don't believe anyone would have believed me. You know in some kind of way I thought my brothers would have been able to save me, but in reality they were little boys about eight, nine, or ten but between you and me, they were big in my heart. They were my brothers, and they were my heroes. I never really wanted my nephew to go, but I wished his father would come get him, but he didn't, he never came. The only time I saw him was when he had something smart to say, always criticizing someone. I don't know what it was about me he didn't like, but it was okay. I loved his son just the same and between me and you I loved him too; it's just that we don't say that too each other in this family; it's taboo.

Over His Dead Body

Tango came home the next morning and couldn't believe what he was told. He thought we made it all up, but when he saw the look on our faces, the worry in my mother's eyes, and my children's bedroom, he knew we weren't kidding. I mean their bedrooms were a mess. I didn't notice it last night, but the children's beds were broken, and their toys were smashed to pieces. Okay, now I'm pissed off. They kept my kids up all night, tore up their bedrooms, and didn't bother to apologize, and to top it off, Quick only needed $2,000 to get out of jail, and my mother was wondering how she could get the money to bail him out.

At first I thought I was hearing things, but I had almost stopped in midair when I heard my mother say to the person on the phone that her name wasn't the only one on the mortgage. Is she kidding me, after all she's been through last night, after what could have happened to my children. I wish I would sign a piece of paper that would allow him to be bailed out of jail. I guess what they say is true, God takes care of fools and children because it didn't take long before he came home. I guess the look still works, and if you knew my mother, you would know the look. My mother have a way of getting you to do something for her even if you don't want to, and don't let her start talking because she is one smooth momma. I mean real smooth, you just have to love her. Once you look at that round face, squishy body, and her soft hands, you can't help but do anything in the world for her, but I had to stand strong, and this time someone else had to fall prey.

When I saw Quick come through the front door, I walked to the back of the house. I figured he would stop in the living room to speak to my mother, but he continued to walk toward my bedroom. He stopped in the dining room and had the nerve to say he was sorry, but he didn't sound as if he meant it, it sound rehearsed. What was he sorry for? Sorry he got caught, sorry he put our mother through last night, or sorry because he is sorry.

Here we go again. I knew it wouldn't take long. A couple of weeks had gone by before I would start seeing new faces in and out of my house. I thought this time he has really lost his mind, Quick had this guy come to the house that he said he knew when he was in prison a few years back. He tried to tell me that this guy was all right, but to me this guy was too quiet, and he looked as if he had a lot of problems. First of all, I didn't trust him. Every time he came to my house, they would go upstairs to the attic, unlock one of the bedroom doors, and sit in that room for hours. Second, I didn't trust him, besides Quick coming and going up into the attic, the little weasel was back and coming and going up to the attic as well. Now what are they up to?

I remember having a conversation with my mother in regard to this new traffic in the house. She told me that this new guy was a friend of Quick's and he came by to help Quick fix his computer. They went so far as to bring this guy's daughter to the house. They said she knows a program that could fix the computer. Okay, if that's what they wanted me to believe, but I knew better than that. This guy looked as if he would blow up a plane in a minute, and his daughter was no older than thirteen. I was fed up with his crap. Did we not have the authorities in this house? Did he understand that they could have seized this house? You know what, damn the house, they could have taken my kids.

We returned to my bedroom so we could discuss what we were going to do about our family, and how close we were into moving out of this house. He got a job on Jamaica Avenue at a women's apparel store as a security guard. I guess he knew I was serious. I wanted us to get away. Surprisingly, he came home each week with a full check cashed. He would only take out enough money for carfare and lunch. The rest was put away for us to move. I guess he wanted to move just as much as I did. He hadn't had a drink in some time, and with all of this confusion, I thought he would have had a drink or two by now, but he was sober, and he was actually standing up for his family, for our family.

Quick must have heard our conversation because he was in the living room ranting and raving. He went on saying that no one was going to do anything to him and no one was going to hurt his mother. I thought to myself, *This guy has got to be kidding*. If anyone was hurting our mother, it was him. Did he notice the look on her face while we were forced to sit in the living room for hours? No, I did. *Did he see her face as they led them out of the house in handcuffs? No, I did.* DID HE SEE HER SHAKING ONCE THEY LEFT THE HOUSE? NO, I DID. So what in the hell was he talking about someone hurting his mother? Last I checked her name is on both of our birth certificates. Well, at least on his. My birth certificate is another story, if that's my real name.

Hit or Miss

We walked out of the bedroom into the living room. I stood by the window, and he sat on the steps, and we listened to everything he said. He went so far as to pull a wad of money out of his pocket and slammed it on the floor. He told my mother that he was not going back to jail for anything. He swore up and down that he was not doing anything wrong. He looked at him sitting on the steps and said that our lives would not be worth one pluck nickel if he went back to jail. Whether he realized it or not, he would be sending himself back to jail, or maybe he should be in jail for the murder of that seventeen-year-old boy who he was supposed to have ordered to be killed over a gold chain. Yes, that's right, over a gold chain.

If anything happens to us, the same would happen to you, and that was my promise. We argued back and forth until my mother yelled. The one with the most sense would shut up. Well, I guess neither one of us had much sense because we both continued to argue until he went back upstairs and we went back into the bedroom. The kids ate their lunch before going to the park. He left for work, and Tango prepared for the overnight shift at the lot. When we returned home from the park I noticed, Quick's girlfriend was in the yard with her kids. They were riding up and down the yard on their motorbikes. The little weasel was sitting in the shade with this stupid smile on his face, as if he was up to something and he probably was up to something. I walked into the house complaining that I smelt something burning. I knew it had something to do with the weasel, after all he was in the backyard sitting in the area close to where the smell was coming from. As I complained to my mother about that odd smell, I told her that the weasel had to go. Well, Quick came out of his bedroom, stood on the front stoop as if he was manning the fort. He heard me complaining to my mother, and he yelled back into the house that the weasel wasn't going anywhere.

Calling the police was a waste of time, so I took the kids back to the park and returned later to give them a bath. They ate their dinner and watched a little TV before they went to bed. I wanted to sit on the front stoop and wait for him to come home from work, but by the time I went outside, it was full of people, and they were making more noise than usual. I'm not surprised the police didn't show up and tell them that they were disturbing the peace, but I guess they have more pressing things do, like eating a few donuts.

The next morning I saw beer bottles, cigarette butts, and half-full bags of potato chips all over the front yard, but I could have cared less we were going to be moving soon, and I am going to get an order to have these people removed from the house. I know my mother is going to fight me on this because he is her son, but the rest of the people are not related to me, and it's time for them to go, especially that little weasel. Things are so bad in the house that I have to put locks on my bedroom door. I would lock up the kids' bedroom, but they wouldn't be able to play in their room when they wanted to, so I put all of their important things in our bedroom and let them play in their bedrooms when they wanted.

Later that day after work, I decided to visit a friend of mine. I guess you could call it a small world because I didn't know that this friend knew Quick and his friends. It made me wonder how much of a friend he really was, but after a few minutes, I knew he was a true friend. He told me to be careful, he told me that Quick had put a hit on me and my family. Yeah, that's right, my brother Quick wanted us out of the way. I guess I was interfering with his business.

About a month had passed and I was still around, but from the look on this guy's face, maybe I shouldn't have been. He was looking at me as if he thought he had seen a ghost. You see, one day I was in the park in South Ozone Queens with my girls from the group home. We decided to take the babies on a picnic because it was such a beautiful day, and the girls deserved a day outdoors. As the girls strolled their infants to the tables, I pulled the food, soda, and chips from the rear of the van. "This seems like a good spot," one of the girls yelled. I guess it was. It was right across from the basketball court and in direct view of all those sweat-driven men and those tight shirts.

As the girls fed their infants, I was reading the weekend log of activities entered by staff. It seems as though the girls had a good weekend without any incident. I felt good about the girls at MIP one and even better because I was the new supervisor of the house. This promotion to supervisor was a nice surprise, and it couldn't have come at a better time. Even though the house was in far rockaway, I loved it. Don't get me wrong, I miss MIP four, but now I got the chance to supervise my own staff and hopefully be a role model for the girls.

I knew I didn't have anything to worry about because I had the best staff in the world, so I sat back and enjoyed the remainder of the day with my girls. Well, I thought I was enjoying my day until I saw this guy approaching me very slow, so I sat up straight and asked him if I could help him. As he got closer, he called my name, and I replied yes. He continued to approach me, so I stood up. He asked me if I remembered him. I honestly did not remember this guy. He mentioned a few names, but I didn't know any of them. Then it clicked that this guy doesn't know me from a can of paint. Okay, is this the guy my brother Quick must have hired to do his dirty work, or is it mistaken identity? But who could mistake my name? It's not a common name, so who the hell was he? He left in a blue Toyota when the girls returned with their babies. At first, I thought it was strange for him to know my name then I remembered what I had been told, is it true? Did Quick put a hit on me and my family?

If It Ain't One Thing, It's Another

Everyone seems to be having a good time, and why shouldn't they? After all, they are living rent-free and running up all the bills. I can't keep robbing Peter to pay Paul, especially when Peter and Paul won't give me the rent money. I went so far as to have the upstairs tenants served with eviction papers so they will be moving out, and as for the tenant on the first floor, she continues to come up with one excuse after another—first it's her son, then it's her sister, now it's some illness. What else is she going to come up with? Well, I'm not going to wait around and see. Right after I talk to the tenant in the basement, I'm going to see my lawyer friend on Queens Boulevard to get her evicted.

Well, that talk never happened. The basement tenant pulled a gun out on him and Tango when they went to talk to her about the rent. If it isn't one thing, it's another. Now why in the hell would she do that? Normally, I would be pissed, but this is family, I raised this child. When I went to the side door, I asked her what was wrong, but all I could hear her say was "Tango, move out of the way." She said she wasn't trying to shoot Tango. Well, then who was she trying to shoot, him or me? I asked her to put the gun down and let's talk. She said no. I couldn't figure it out. What happened? I saw her yesterday, and everything seemed to be just fine. I asked her, was anyone in there with her? She said that her boyfriend was at the store and her daughter was in the room. Well, at least she is talking to me. I asked her if anyone was hurt. She said no. Again I asked her to put the gun down and let's talk. This time there was no answer. All I heard was footsteps going down the steps, so I walked away from the side door and called 911.

I never thought they would arrest her, but she was in possession of a gun. I knew something wasn't right, but I couldn't put my finger on it. A few minutes later an officer came from the side of the house holding her daughter's hand.

They got to be kidding. What is going on? She was putting this child in the police car, and they were on their way to child protective services. I called to the officer and told her that this was my niece and the women they were arresting were also my niece it was her mother they were arresting. I told the officer that I will take her with me. They turned to her mother, and she said she wanted her daughter to go with me. At this point I was really confused. This girl just pulled a gun on me, and now she is saying it is okay for her daughter to come with me. No really what is going on? Did I miss something? Before I knew it, that boyfriend of hers came walking up the block. Maybe he would be able to shed some light on what was going on. When I asked him about this, he acted like he had just arrived, but you could clearly see that he knew something, but what, I don't know. He had the nerve to tell me that he would take my niece with him after they drove off with her mother. Are you kidding me? She wasn't going anywhere with him, and he was not going back into that house. If looks could kill, I would be dead twice over. He wanted to get back into the house, but for what? What was in there that he needed to get? Well, too bad, he wasn't going back in there, and as a matter of fact, we couldn't go in the house either. The police searched the house and told us to lock it up. I don't know if they found anything in there, and if they did, they weren't going to tell us, so we locked up the basement and left.

To make the day go by a little faster, we fed all the kids and rented some movies for the kids. Later that day the three of us tried to figure out what we were going to do and how were we going to get her out of jail so she wouldn't lose custody of her child. It was barely 6:30 in the morning when Coffee came knocking on my bedroom door asking what happened. Okay, here we go, first someone to blame, then the tears, next where is my granddaughter, and lastly, the famous "I'll be back."

Well, that went well. One thing I could say about Coffee is, she is consistent. Imagine her helping us figure out what to do about her daughter being arrested and having a gun. Better yet, imagine her helping me with her granddaughter. It's all the same, she will stay with us until we find out what is going on with her mother, but that didn't take long, her mother is here. Now maybe she could tell me what happened yesterday. Well, excuse me. No thank you, no explanation, nothing. She came in and collected her daughter without even batting her eyes. They'll need me again, and this time they will be on their own. Who am I kidding? God doesn't' like ugly, and he cares too little for ignorance.

A Reasonable Doubt

What is wrong now? I barely walked into my front yard when I noticed detectives were all over the place. The only difference this time was that it was broad daylight, and it wasn't the NYC police. It was New Jersey homicide detectives. They were in the garage, the barbeque pit, behind the bus, and around the house digging in the dirt. There was even more going on inside the house. What they were looking for, I don't know, but the items to be searched for were as follows:

Trace evidence including but not limited to

fibers; hairs; blood; saliva; fingerprints; palm prints; photos of scenes; a map; weapons including blunt instruments; a wallet and contents; evidence of the planning of the described crime including but not limited to writings, documents, and video and audio tapes, phone records, computer or electronic messaging and storage systems; evidence of the relationship between the involved parties; and any other evidence of this crime that a thorough search will reveal.

You know it was as if they knew which rooms to search. They searched the front room, the basement, and my bedroom. What I hoped they didn't find in my bedroom, they did—the herbs. They were in my drawer, and not surprisingly, the detectives called me into the bedroom and asked me what was it? I wanted to say, "What do you think?" I'm just about done with the police. Every time you turn around, they are at my house, but when I call them, they are nowhere to be found. Before I could get another word out of my mouth, the detective put my stuff back in the draw and said that they were done searching my bedroom. Next they went into the kitchen, the backroom, and the pantry.

Then all of a sudden, I heard an officer say, "Right here." At first I didn't know what he meant by right here because I was too busy making sure they put all of my stuff back in the draw. I called my sister Beauty and asked her to pick my kids up from school so they would not have to go through this again, but it was too late. They were already en route to the house.

Beauty was at their school and explained what was going on, so the school principal called the bus company, who got in touch with the driver of the bus and was informed to pull over and give location. Beauty caught up with the bus and removed them. I asked them to take them to my girlfriend Worthy's house. She only lived a few blocks away from me. She kept them there until everyone was gone. Before I knew it, they were packing up what they had seized from the house, even the weight out of the dining room window.

I later realized what they carried in that black bag had to be something heavy. The windows in the dining room had chains attached on both sides, it held the weights in the window. What I found to be odd was that they removed one weight from one of the windows and left the others. This left the window a lot easier to slide up and down, it also made it easier to break. Hmm, something wasn't right. After living in this house for almost forty years and sitting in that window, the one window that was the hardest to open was all of a sudden the easiest to open. They took that weight! And that's what must have been in that black bag. But why would they choose that particular window? With all the windows in the, house they chose that window. The only windows in the house with weights were the ones in the dining room. It puzzles me, and it should puzzle you too. How did they know there were weights in those windows, and why would they take that one weight over the other?

Once again our lives was turned upside down, only this time they didn't touch my children's bedroom, nor did it last all night. The search and cleanup ended around six, maybe seven o'clock. The kids came home from Worthy's house. They took their baths and ate their dinner before playing games and going to bed. Okay, now what? It was hard to go to work the next day knowing the police conducted a cavity search on my house. Sometimes I didn't want to come home from work because I didn't know what to expect. By now it became the norm, I would come home from work or school and have men in black—oops, my bad—men in blue in my house. When everyone else is teaching their kids not to talk to strangers, how to cross the street by looking both ways, I was too busy teaching my children how to play dead. They were told if they came home from school and saw the front shade pulled down, then they are to go up the street to Worthy's house and wait for me there. Can you believe it? When most mothers are teaching their children safety measures like don't play with matches, how to stop, drop, and roll. I was teaching my children the unthinkable. I know it sounds crazy, but what other choice did we have?

Things were getting out of control around here, so we decided to walk away with whatever savings we had, along with the clothes on our backs and our children. We were going to sell both homes and start all over. To tell you the truth, it will probably kill both of us, after all I grew up in my house, and he grew up in his house. The hardest part of it all is telling my mother. I know she is not going to like it, but what other choice do I have? I spoke to a realtor who came by the house to talk with my mother and me. She told us that she could have the house listed on the MLS list by the end of the week, and of course, my mother didn't like it. Well, I didn't like it either, but what was she expecting me to do? Something had to give, it was either them, me, or the house, and by the way things were going, it looks as if it was my family that would be paying the price.

Of course Quick put in his two cents, he told my mother that she didn't have to sell the house and that he would help her pay the bills. He has got to be kidding me—help pay the bills. Damn, he's not helping me pay the bills now, he's just creating them. He had the nerve to say he would buy me out. I just looked at my mother. Where did she think he was going to get the money from? If he had that kind of money, then why don't he move out and leave us alone, and just as I thought, we couldn't sell the house. My mother said she wasn't going to sign the contract to sell. I don't feel like taking this to court, but if I have to, I will.

This was the first time in a long time that I came home from work and found the house quiet. The kids were at camp, and he was at work. As for everyone else, they weren't around. I walked into the house and found out that they arrested Quick. I didn't know what to think except who was going to be here to take care of my mother. I know God doesn't like ugly, but I truly hope he is looking the other way because I was relieved when I heard the weasel was arrested. To my understanding, they also arrested this flunky who lived in our neighborhood. As a matter of fact, he went to school with my oldest brother Phar.

Nothing seemed to be making sense. The more I asked questions, the more complicated things became. For one, I was told these guys murdered someone who lived in New Jersey. They said he was an ex-police officer who was injured and was supposed to spend the rest of his life in a wheelchair. To make things worse, he was the lover to the wife of the guy who my brother Quick had come to the house. If I remember his daughter was here to fix the computer that Quick had up in the attic. I was also told that his wife and that guy had a bad drug habit and his wife had promised her husband that she would stay clean.

That was supposed to be the reason he took his wife back, but that was not my problem. As least I thought it wasn't. But it soon became a big problem. You see, the next day Tango was arrested for the murder of this man as well. He too was taken to the New Jersey prison. The house was truly empty this time, even Quick's girlfriend and kids disappeared.

I can't believe it. The family name is in the paper, including our address. New Jersey sure doesn't waste any time putting all your business out there. Without a reasonable doubt, they already have him guilty. I guess the trial was a waste of time, and it was a waste of my time as well. They knew my testimony wasn't going to help Tango. They had it all set up from the very beginning. First, I received a phone call from Tango's lawyer (a legal aid lawyer) asking me to testify on Tango's behalf, then Quick's girlfriend called me and asked me if I was still getting high school diplomas for people because she needed one. I told her I don't do things like that, then I hung up on her. What I should have told her was that "yeah, she could get one." Just like I did by graduating from high school.

Did she not think that I knew what she was trying to do. She was helping them discredit me so I could not speak on Tango's behalf. First of all, I don't do things like that. Second, I knew the conversation was being taped. Can you believe it? The state's attorney/DA (whatever they call themselves) would do anything to win their case, and third, Tango's lawyer asked me to meet her a half hour before the trial. We met in the hallway of the courthouse, and she told me that she was going to brief me on the questions she was going to ask me when I took the stand. She said she wanted me to be sure of my answers. She also told me to be prepared for questioning by the DA. She said they could be difficult and twist things around, and most of the time they would make you feel as though you were the one on trial.

What I should have prepared myself for was her lies. She didn't ask me any of the questions we talked about in the hallway before the trial. She didn't object to any of the questions they asked me. For instance, they wanted to know what I did for a living. Before I could tell him that I was a life skills specialist and I wanted to go to school to be an international judge, the DA interrupted me and said maybe what I did for a living was to go around beating people up like my brothers. You would think Tango's lawyer would object, but instead the judge told me not to answer, and he warned the DA about his remarks. Quick wasn't in the courthouse, but they did ask me questions about him as well. At this point I knew they were trying to get me to choose one brother over the other. They also wanted me to turn on Tango, but it wasn't about turning on Tango, it was about telling the truth, and the truth of the matter was, I just wanted this nightmare to be over, and I wanted my brothers back. The same brothers that took apples from the apple tree, the same brothers that would run the streets playing team tag until midnight, and the same brothers that would run and get the biggest and thickest switch off the tree when they knew someone was going to get lit up for doing something they had no business doing. Those are the brothers I needed and the brothers I missed.

It was Quick's turn to take the stand, so they brought him out the back. I guess that's where they held witnesses that were already in custody. He looked around, and he noticed our mother cousin, brother Phar, and me sitting in the courtroom. They asked him about his involvement in the murder. At that time the court room got real quiet even the cell phones were silent. But believe it or not, Quick had a heart, I felt it sinking. I don't know if it was because he saw me crying, or was it that he felt our mother's heart dying? He admitted he had immunity to testify against his own brother. He also admitted he had immunity with the murder of that seventeen-year-old boy. Quick admitted he ordered the hit on this guy. He said that his friend could not concentrate on what they was supposed to be doing because he was having problems with his wife who he assumed was cheating on him. So in order for them to move forward with what they were doing, they had to get rid of the problem, but what they was supposed to do from what I heard was that they was supposed to hurt this guy not eliminate him.

He never admitted it, but word had it that Quick set the whole thing up. He is a genius. This sounds like something that would happen in the movies. Quick was already a two-time loser, and if he went to jail again, he would be spending the rest of his life there. What came out during and after the testimonies was that on several different occasions, Quick got the flunky from our neighborhood and the little weasel to go to New Jersey to find this man, but each time they went, they could not find him. Quick's patients were running thin, and the husband was getting frustrated that his wife continued the affair, so in order to find the exact location, the husband followed his wife to this man's house.

From the testimony of the little weasel, he testified that when they found this man, he stomped this guy until he gurgled. From the testimony of the flunky, he testified that the rain was pouring down so bad that it was hard for him to drive back home. He said he could barely see the roads. He stated that his van was parked a couple of cars away from where this guy was being stomped. He also testified that he saw Tango raise his right hand and hit this guy with an object.

Call me stupid or just plain dumb, but why didn't Tango's lawyer question the flunky when he made those statements. For one, how could he see which hand Tango was using if he said that the rain was pouring down and he could hardly see out his van window? Two, if an autopsy was done on this man to show his cause of death, it should have also showed the angle of the blunt object that supposedly caused this fatal blow. Tango is left handed, and if he had struck a blow with his dominant hand, then the angle would be much different than the angle of a person who would have used the opposite hand.

Imagine using your dominant hand to hammer a nail into a piece of plywood right after your boss told you that you were fired. How hard do you think you could swing that hammer? Correct, nine times out of ten you are aiming straight for your target and hitting it each time you swung. Now imagine you are using your other hand and your boss told you that you were fired. Nine times out of ten, you are going to miss that target and either strike the wood leaving half moon marks from the hammer in the wood, or you would injure your hand once that hammer hit the wood. Shoot, you might even drop the hammer and stop swinging. Why didn't his lawyer bother to see how many times this man was struck? She didn't check the angle in which he was struck nor did she check to see if Tango's hands had any old wombs, and what about checking the ground for any marks made during the scuffle. This puts a reasonable doubt in my mind.

It was said that Quick had to show the husband some kind of proof that this guy got the message to leave his wife alone, but things went a little too far. Quick did have proof, one form of proof was the weight in the window. It was supposed to be the weight that caused his death. There was also mention of a wallet that was taken off this guy's person as proof that they made contact with him. Come to find out. What I suspected as an odd smell coming from my backyard that day I saw the little weasel sitting and smiling was actually the little weasel burning the wallet. He burned it, and the police found it.

Tango never took the stand, nor did he give them any evidence, but the DNA was full of it. You know what I mean—Dem No good Attorneys. They knew they didn't have anything on him: no blood, fibers, or fingerprints. Wait, I take that back. Yes, they could have found Tango's prints on it, they could have even found mine, yours and anyone else who came to that house and sat in that window. We all sat in that window as kids and pushed those weights back and forth. Shoot we even got yelled at for touching the weights in the windows.

I wanted to die when they sentenced Tango to thirty years. What am I supposed to do without him. He was my right arm. I thought I was hearing things when I heard they gave the flunky five years and the weasel ten, but when they handed the husband twenty-five years, I knew something was wrong but what about the business they had in the attic, it was a shop up there, I mean computers and plates to make counterfeit money. I remember being called into the bedroom and asked to take care of my mother because Quick wasn't going to be around for a while. I thought Quick was telling me that he was going to jail, but when he showed me those plates, I thought I was going to lose my mind. Was he kidding me? Did he not know that it was against the law? Calling the police at this point didn't make any sense because they were probably on his payroll, besides Quick was getting what he deserved. He was going to have to live with what has happened to his brother for the rest of his life, and believe it or not, he almost seems remorseful. The tone in his voice had changed, and he looked at me as if he was asking me to guard his most treasured treasure, our mother.

Am I My Brother's Keeper

It was hard going home without him. It was even harder telling my kids that Uncle Tango was going to be away for a while, but not a day went by without the kids talking about Uncle Tango. I thought with everyone out of the house except for my family and my mother, things were going to be quiet, but it wasn't. The kids were acting up in school, and he was drinking more and more, so much that he lost his job. It was hard working, caring for the kids, my mother, bills, and the tenants. If Tango were here, things would be a lot easier. Tango would sit and play cards with my mother, and whenever he got paid, he would give me money to help pay the bills. My mother decided she would like to have a home attendant, and at this point, I think she was right. The only problem we were having was finding the right home attendant. As a matter of fact, she had several home attendants before we could find the right one.

Truth's school called me while I was at work and told me that my son was taken to the hospital and I should meet them there. Well, I left work and arrived at the hospital, but I couldn't find him. I searched every place—the emergency room, ICU, the children's unit, and even the trauma unit, but no Truth. I tried calling his school back, but they were closed, so I called home, and my mother told me that Truth called and asked for me. My mother told him that I was on my way to get him. At that point she said that a nurse had informed her where my son was in the hospital. They said he was in child psych, and I should ask for that unit when I come to visit. I said visit. What are they talking about, I am coming to get my son.

I arrived on the psych ward for children and demanded to see my son. I was told that I could not see him because they were having dinner and that his doctor would like to see me. I asked, "What doctor, and why is he here?" I was told he got into an altercation in school and threatened another student and staff. "You got to be kidding me." I demanded they release my son, and they told me that they could not release him because he was under observation. "Observation for what, and who ordered an observation? I want my son released right now." Well, of course they called security, and I was escorted out of the hospital. I was told that visiting hours were over and I could revisit him the next day. I told them I had not seen my son and that I wanted to see him now. They had three security guards walk me over to the visiting area, and I saw Truth, he looked fine to me. So what were they talking about? He was playing with the other kids, and he asked me if he could go home. I explained to him that they would not let me take him home, but I will be there the next day, and he will come home with me. I was told that I should not tell him that he would be coming home the next day. "Well, I don't have to tell you what I told them? & %$< #@ %&#! $* I'm getting my son tomorrow." I left that place in tears. "Just who in the #&** do they think they are? They have no idea who they are %*$#@&! with."

ACS, the Agency for Children Services, is the first place I went to the next morning. I told them what had happened and they sent a worker out with me to the hospital. I couldn't wait to see them and Truth, and especially that doctor. How dare they stop me from seeing my son! When we arrived, I heard my son's mouth all the way down the hall, saying, "Let me out of here." When I saw him, he started yelling even louder. His eyes were glossy, and he was sweating. This boy even started cursing. He was so mad I couldn't calm him down, so I rang the bell and the counselor came to the door. I told her I was coming to get my son. She told me that I couldn't get my son. She also told me that ACS has the case.

They told me that I could not see my son unless it was visiting hours. Well, to their surprise they thought the woman with me was a friend or a family member. They had no idea who she was. I never introduced her, and she stood there without saying a word, until she heard them lie and say that ACS has the case. She showed her identification and informed them that she was ACS and that they do not have my case. So they had to release my son. They were also told that they had no business keeping my son or admitting him into the hospital. My son was released within minutes. I asked him if he was all right. He said that they gave him some medication for his asthma. You and I both know that was not right, he had no asthma attack.

Just as we found a new school for Truth, Justice decided she wanted to be an actress. She started acting out in school, and again, I was in the principal's office. They say she threatened a teacher. Well, as I got to the bottom of things, I found out the teacher was talking about her younger brother Wise. Justice said she overheard the teachers talking and this particular teacher who she had in the first grade was telling another teacher that if Wise was anything like Justice then she would not want him in her class. She also said that Justice was a handful and had an answer for everything. Now let's stop right there. First of all, this teacher had no business talking about my children. Second, they should not be discussing anything regarding children or their behaviors in a public area or with another teacher unless there is a conference being held and the parent is involved. Third, she should be glad Justice only threatened her, not to say Justice was right, but what did she think would have happened to her if I had overheard the conversation?

I had to figure something out. The bills are starting to pile up, and I needed some extra cash, and the only thing I could do was to get back to the oldest profession in the world, braiding hair. I figured if I charge $150 for single braids and $90 for cornrows, I could make some extra money and pay my bills at the same time. I could really make some money if I have to add extensions, and of course if they wanted invisible cornrows, then the price would be much higher. I even thought about selling my hair grease for anyone's hair that is damaged, but it takes too long to make the grease, and the kids don't like the smell of the grease as it is being made, but it makes the hair grow; at least it makes my hair grow.

"Look, miss, I have more than one brother. I don't know what they do, or who they do, as a matter of fact, how did you get my phone number?" I received a phone call from the Department of Social Services in Central Islip regarding foster care and adoption. The worker informed me that my brother's daughter was in foster care and was going to be adopted. She mentioned before she could be adopted the agency would have to have tried every reasonable effort to locate family members, and that's when they came across my mother's name. The agency must have gotten this information from the hospital, but who was the mother? Better question, who was the father?

Okay, now that the mystery was solved and I know which brother decided to reproduce, it was my brother Self. I was told she was born in the ambulance and weighed one pound. They lived in this apartment complex, and the information from the rental office had my mother listed as next to kin, this led them to my mother, which brought them to me. To make a long story short, they asked me if I wanted custody of my niece. I told them yes. We didn't believe in placing our family in foster care. The worker asked me questions, and then I asked her questions regarding my niece like what is her name. She told me her name is Heaven. Then came some bad news according to this worker. She said Heaven would need to be turned several times during the night. She mentioned she would bleed if you touched her. Next, I was told she was blind and that she was on a special formula because she had an eating disorder. Well, if she thought that was going to make me say, "I didn't want her," she was wrong. It was just the opposite, I couldn't want her more.

I was to attend a permanency hearing the following week after the worker did a home visit. As I met her at my front door, she looked at me as if she had already made up her mind. She assumed the worst. She had her pad and pen out and began writing. It took all but two seconds to figure out that she was not feeling this placement for my niece. I showed her the living room, dining room, and kitchen. As we started down the basement steps, out of nowhere she mentioned there would not be any kinship care or foster care stipend. Okay. (And what? I don't remember asking for any money.) She told me she needed to see the children's bedrooms and the bed and space where Heaven would be sleeping.

You don't know how relieved I was that she didn't go down the basement steps. The boiler was not working, and you could see the holes in the ceiling where it was leaking from the kitchen sink. I was also happy that I was able to put up some ceiling tile in the dining room so she couldn't see the leaks from the bathroom into the dining room. I know it was deceiving, but do you honestly think she would have accepted the fact that I was getting the leaks fixed. I don't believe she wanted me to have custody of my niece. All she did was talk about how well the foster mother was taking care of her, and how well she is doing even though she had several challenges. You know I'm glad to hear she was doing so well, truly I am, but that's not what she was here for. She was here to do a family assessment, so assess.

She saw my children's bedroom, and with a stern face, she mentioned she did not see a crib for my niece, so I took her down the hall. There she saw a white crib dressed in white bedding, matching curtains on the windows, a dresser with a lamp, a floor-length mirror, and several stuffed animals propped in a chair. She was speechless. There was nothing left for her to say. To complete the showing, I showed her my bedroom. She saw nothing unusual about my bedroom except a cradle in the corner of my bedroom. It was oval, white and iron, with white eyelet bedding. It was beautiful as a matter of fact it was the same one I used for all my children. She seemed pleased, but it didn't mean that she was going to rule in my favor. I was beginning to wonder if she heard about all the things that happened in the house because if she did, I could forget it. I knew they were not going to let Heaven stay, and who could blame them? Half the time, I don't even want to stay here.

I received a letter in the mail telling me when I was to appear in court, so I prepared for court. That morning as I was ironing my clothes Self came walking up the steps, I knew he was going to be released from prison soon, but I didn't know it was going to be today. I didn't know whether I should be happy to see him or what. The last time I saw him he was walking up the yellow line in the middle of the street, so I called him and asked him what was he doing. He had tears in his eyes, and all he kept saying was that he was going to kill Phar because he did him wrong. Our own brother he was trying to kill him, and for what? What happened now? From what I was told, he was upset with Phar about some girl that he liked. He said Phar dissed him and his girlfriend. To tell you the truth, whatever Phar said, it was probably the truth. I'm sorry, but Self has a habit of picking these girls that look like ten miles of rough road, but not in this case, this girl was really nice and beautiful inside and out, but again she had baggage.

Self came into the house with this blank look on his face. I'm surprised he spoke. At first I wasn't going to say anything to him, but I decided to tell him about Heaven, and he asked me if I didn't mind if he came along. I knew he had that look on his face for some reason and I'm quite sure he already knew about the court date. He was probably trying to make it here before I went to court, and he was probably living in a halfway house, and they let him come out for the day due to court, so he didn't have to act as if he knew nothing, but then that's Self. He usually knows nothing.

We spoke on the ride up to Central Islip, which was easier than I thought. Self kept babbling about getting his life together, and if I heard it once, I heard it twice. Self and I used to be real close. I thought he was the polite brother. He had a lot of manners and always dressed with a shirt and tie. He even had a job at the hotel with our father. I remember this one time when Self was dating this girl who also worked at the hotel, say to her there was more fish in the sea. Then there was this time when he brought this chick home who had more tattoos than I cared to count. Some would call her trailer trash, but to me she was young and dumb, and he knew it. As we continued the conversation, I told him that the decision was going to be up to the judge, but after the judge listens to the social worker's testimony, he will probably rule nonsuitable placement.

Do You Swear to Tell the Truth

" I do." The judge read the worker's report after I was sworn in. He asked the worker if the residence had enough space for Heaven. The worker and I looked at each other and began to laugh. We had more than enough space especially since everyone else was gone. I knew at that point the judge was going to deny my petition. I knew we shouldn't have laughed, and by the look on the judge's face, he did not look amused. He asked us what was so funny because he would also like to laugh. So the worker told him that the house has eleven bedrooms. He then turned to me and asked if he could move into the home. The judge was informed that Self was present in the court house so he requested Self to come to the hearing. He looked surprised as he was sworn in. He looked at me first, then he looked at the worker. The judge asked him a few questions, and to my surprise, he told the judge he would like for me to have custody of Heaven. He told the judge that he was not prepared to care for her at this time.

The judge was ready to rule, but before he did, the judge informed Self that he no longer had rights to his daughter nor could he make any decisions that were to be made regarding the well-being of Heaven. He was also informed that if I wanted to move out of the state or the country with her, I could do so. I was awarded full custody of Heaven. We left the courthouse and were told by the worker to meet her at DSS. This is where they will do the transition. We were taken into this room and waited for about two hours. Just then, another worker had told us that the foster mother did not take it well. We were told that the foster mother fell out into the street when she received the news that she was to turn Heaven over to the worker. When Heaven arrived, the worker proceeded to give her to me, but I asked her to give her to her father first. I didn't want to seem selfish. No matter what has happened or what may happen, he is still her father, but he needs to keep in mind that I took an oath with the court and to myself, so in the best interest of this child, I will protect and shield her from harm.

Self moved back into the house, he got a good job and was even paying rent. I couldn't believe it, he was actually being a good dad, he even brought his oldest daughter Iyleah to the house. She was about two years old and was living with her maternal aunt out in Long Island. She stayed for a couple of days, and then he took her back to her aunt in Long Island. This continued throughout the summer, until it got to the point when Self would drop Iyleah off to the house, and he would disappear for several days. He continued this for several weeks, mostly when I was at work. He would show up and disappear. The next time I saw Iyleah without Self, I called the aunt and asked her to come and get Iyleah because I didn't want to get caught up in whatever mess Self was creating. I was totally shocked when she told me that Self had told her that he was working and planning on getting custody of his kids, so he could raise them together. Well, what a surprise. I knew he was up to something, it was just a matter of time before he showed his true colors. I didn't go to work that morning because I waited for him to sneak in the house, and since he didn't see my car, I guess he figured I wasn't home. It may have been my mouth he heard before he even saw me, but by then it was too late for him to turn around because his daughter had already called his name out.

I asked him what he was doing with his daughter, and of course, he came up with this story that he was getting an apartment with his girlfriend up the street and they were going to live together. Don't get me wrong, it's nice that the sisters are getting to know one another and will be raised near each other, but is he ready for this? Does he know what this entails? I hope he knows once he gets custody of her there is no turning back, and I wish him all the luck in the world. He said he had a plan, so I left for work, but when I came home, she was still there, and he was gone, and as a matter of fact, he was gone for several days, and he didn't pay his rent this month.

I walked up the street to the girl's house he was supposed to be staying with, and this woman came to the door. I recognized her instantly and prayed this wasn't the person he was talking about. I couldn't stand her. She was trash-talking then, and she is trash-talking now. She said hello, and I said hello. She asked if I was looking for Self, and I told I was. She had this little smirk on her face as she told me he walked to the store with her daughter, with her daughter! Okay, when he comes back tell him to come to his sister's house so he can walk to the park with his daughters. She couldn't wait to tell me that they were out getting things for their apartment and the baby shower. What baby shower? Is he kidding me? Has he completely lost his mind? He's getting too old for this and so am I.

My mother was watching the kids as they were playing in the yard. I on the other hand was in the basement packing Self's things and preparing for an argument. This was not going to happen to me again, and no offense, I love my niece, but he is going to have to take her back to her maternal aunt and find another place to stay. Better yet, I'll call her myself and ask her to come and get Iyleah. Well, that went well. Self told her that he would be taking care of his daughter and that he thanked her for caring for Iyleah, taking care of Iyleah! Taking care of her where, and with what? He already owes me this month's rent, and from what I've been told, he was borrowing money to help with the baby shower, but he couldn't pay me my rent. I wasn't going through this again, having another relative living with me and not pay any rent. Just wait until I see him. As a matter of fact, he will probably come in here with that blank look on his face and have no money. He will play with his kids, and have no money, talk to my mom, and still have no money, he will then ask where I am, and still-have-no-money, he might even thank me for watching his daughter, but guess what he still will not have my money.

I have less than ten words for him. "Where is my money? And oh yeah, get out!" Okay, I'm ready, where is he? I hear him upstairs moving about. He should be making his way downstairs any minute. You know what, never mind, I'll go upstairs to him. It will probably be easier this way. His bags will be upstairs, and he'll be closer to the front door. I could see by the expression on my mother's face that something was wrong. She said his friend was waiting outside for him and they left. Okay, that was a little easier than I had thought, but they are gone, and all I could say was that I hope he had a safe place for his daughter. Of course he did, he left her in the yard playing with the rest of the kids.

Okay, let me understand this, the aunt will not take her back. I don't know where her mother is, and Self just left. I'm being punk'd. I have to be. God wouldn't do this to me again. You have to help me on this one, Lord. Right now I have six children. None of the tenants want to pay their rent at either house. I am trying to keep my job, and on top of everything else, he's not working, and the welfare is giving me a hard time. Lord, I am trying not to lose my mind. I don't need you to point me in the right direction any more, just push me there.

I guess this is where he wants me to be, right back in front of another judge. One would think I was getting money for these kids, but I'm not. I was told the city of New York stopped foster kinship a long time ago. Besides, the last thing I need is for some social worker to be all up and through my business. Not only will they take them away from me, but they will probably take my kids away from me as well, especially after all of the crap that happened in my mother's house. Maybe if I explained things, they would understand. Who am I kidding? They will never understand, the only thing they are interested in is getting into your business and going through your things. I know, I saw Claudine.

I spend more time in court than I do any other place. I finally made the time to petition the court so I could evict all the tenants. I found out the tenant on the first floor was withholding my mail from the mortgage company. I would have changed the address, but I needed to show proof of address so the kids could go to the school in that neighborhood. She was trying to own the house. I contacted the bank and found out the tenant sent several letters to the mortgage company complaining that I have tenants living in the basement and have illegal activities going on in the upstairs apartment. This was one desperate woman. I ran into her former landlord who mentioned he was happy that he finally evicted her. He also said that she caused a lot of confusion with his family and owed him several months rent. Well, she was behind in her rent to me as well. I went to court with her before, and the judge gave her six months to locate another place to live.

As for the tenants upstairs, they were trying to sue me. They even tried to have me arrested for illegal eviction. The upstairs tenants called the police and reported I changed the locks and would not allow her to reenter the apartment. Yes, the locks were changed. However, the locks on the front door were the only locks that were changed, and the tenant on the first floor had reported an intruder, so I changed the locks. I gave the tenant on the first floor a key. The tenant on the second floor had not been there for several days, so I left her a note and several phone messages to come to my house and pick up the key. A couple of days had gone by before I heard from the second floor tenant. She was getting out of a car in front of my house, but when I looked again, she had the police behind her. They put the handcuffs on me and told me that I was being arrested for illegally locking my tenant out of her apartment. I was headed down the stairs when the female officer informed me that I could not lock the tenant out of the house. I explained to the officer that I did not lock the tenant out of the house, I merely changed the lock because of a reported break-in reported by the downstairs tenant. I was able to show them the police report and a copy of the note I left for the tenant telling her to come to my house to pick up her copy of the key. I was released on the spot, and the key was given to the tenant. Come to find out the tenant's son was the intruder. She let him stay there without letting the downstairs tenant know someone would be staying upstairs while she was away. She was evicted several weeks later.

Coffee, her daughter, and granddaughter had moved back into the house. Her daughter was pregnant again, and the idea was for Coffee to help her daughter after she had given birth. They took the rooms in the attic, and my nephew took the basement. Now I know what the Cos meant in that episode when he told his wife that no more people were going to move into their house. Okay, one more person did move into the house. It was my nephew's girlfriend. She told me she was eighteen, but something was telling me that she was not, and that something was her grandfather. He was cool, but was he right? Was she under the age of eighteen or did her mother throw her out of their house.

Like Thieves in the Night

Surprisingly, everyone was getting along, and believe it or not, they were paying their rent, or maybe I spoke to soon. Coffee was starting to complain about everything—the heat in the house, the dishes, the noise is too loud for her granddaughter. Her daughter had another little girl, and you would think this was the first baby ever to hear noise. Coffee was walking around the house telling people they were talking too loud. She would complain that it was either too hot or too cold. What were they, the three bears? If things weren't bad enough, the court postponed the court date, so that meant I will not get rent for two more months from the tenant on the first floor. I know this is the land of the free, but free rent is not part of the deal.

It was always nice to get a letter from Tango. He always knew how to cheer me up even if it felt as though he was a million miles away. If I could change places with him, I would in a heartbeat. I miss him so much, and I know he misses Tango too. I know it's not funny, but when he comes into the house after drinking all day, knowing I'm going to be upset, he opens the basement door as if Tango were down there. Sometimes I wonder what he would do if I didn't tell him that Tango wasn't down there. Would he keep going down the steps and talk as if Tango was there, or would he stay down there all night to sober up? Tango had a way of talking to me so I wouldn't be totally upset with him, and I guess he realized the next day that Tango couldn't help him anymore, so he got up the next morning and showered. He got dressed and went out looking for a job. I barely said a word to him, and he knew what that look meant. I got if from my momma. Don't come back without a job!

By the time I came from work, I was too tired to even read the mail, but one letter stood out and that was from the water company. I read pass all the mumbo jumbo in the letter and noticed it was a $3,000 water bill. From all the leaking pipes, people running water all times of the day, not to mention washing one shirt in the washing machine, no wonder the water bill is high. When I told the rest of the family about the water bill, they acted like I wasn't talking to them, and I guess I wasn't. They already had plans. Coffee was on the phone talking to Phar and Melo about moving. Should I be happy or what? I guess or what? I'm the one that will be stuck paying the bill. For the next few weeks, all I heard was talk about moving and packing and buying new furniture when they get there. At first I thought it was all talk until they came back from down south. They were down south looking for a place to live.

They told my mother that it was a three-bedroom townhouse with a backyard, new washer and dryer, and central air-conditioning. The bottom line was this, my mother, sister, her daughter, and grandchildren were moving, not just out of the house but out of the state. Should I be pissed that they were leaving me with the bills and a run-down house that they, along with all the other siblings and their families, helped tear up, or should I be jumping for joy that I will finally have my house to myself. Well, the next few days couldn't come fast enough. The U-haul truck was parked in the driveway, and I could have sworn I saw a flying chair. The way they were throwing things in that truck, you would have thought they were on a game show called *Load That Truck*.

It is official, everyone is gone, my nephew and his girlfriend even left. I think he went to stay with his mother or sister. Anyway, the house is empty and it's quiet. The next day I came from work and couldn't believe my eyes he was sitting on the stoop watching the kids play in the yard. Now that was a first. We agreed he would be home and help get the house back in order and make sure the kids get home from school until we could figure out how we are going to repair this home and rent out the other home. I tried to get a second mortgage, but my income wasn't enough, besides this house needed too many repairs, and I couldn't do anything with the other home until I evicted the other tenants.

He had this look on his face that wasn't right. I asked him what was wrong, and he said the lights were not working. I asked him if he checked the circuit breaker box, and he said he did. He said that was not the problem, then what is? He found the electric bill, and that the electric bill was $2,000. If the bill was not brought up to date by last week, then the lights would be shut off. He told me that he found the bill while cleaning up and it was open. That bill was dated for the week before last, so that meant that someone knew about the bill. On top of the water bill being $3,000, the electric bill was $2,000. I guess I would have left like I stole something too if I knew I was about to be put out or would have to live in the dark without any water.

The boiler is not working, there is no heat and hot water in the house, and it's starting to get cold at night. Instead of eating something hot, the kids had to sit around a table with candles while eating hamburgers and french fries while wearing their jackets. That night we got all the blankets together, the kids slept in one room, and we had to put pots on the top of the stove to keep the house warm. We took turns and sat up all night checking on the kids and making sure the pots were filled with water. I learned this while growing up in this very same house when the boiler would go out. We would put large pots of water on the stove and open up the oven door. We had to sit up all night to make sure the kids were warm and the pots were filled. We went so far as to iron the kids bed sheets so their beds would be warm before they went to bed.

The next day I went to the welfare and asked for assistance, but I was turned down. I found out that the house had a lien on it from a prior one-shot deal that occurred over twenty years ago. That's right a one-shot deal is when you own a house and you ask social services for assistance. If they grant you that assistance, then they place a lien on your home. You cannot sell that home unless you pay off that grant. I guess that first grant was never paid off. Well, the children living in the home now were not alive when that agreement was made, and I was a child myself.

This is one day I know the kids were happy to go to school. At least they would be warm and have something to eat, not to say there wasn't any food in the house, but at least they could enjoy their meal. We went to the electric company and were able to work out an arrangement. I gave them a down payment and explained the circumstances. What they did for me was allow me to place the bill in his name. We were told that the lights should be on within twenty-four hours, but the worker said that she was going to try and get them on as soon as possible.

Never Give Up

Things were finally starting to look up again. My Sweetie had told me about this lender who could help us with both homes, so I called him, and he agreed to meet with us on Saturday. We had the phones shut off and were only using our cell phones. We were trying to find ways of cutting cost. The next day he drove me to work after dropping the kids off at school and daycare. I believe we were both in a good mood. The lights had come on that morning, and he had a job interview. He was looking pretty good too. He hadn't been drinking, and the kids were happy, that's all that mattered to me. On my way to work, we stopped by the other house to pick up any mail that wasn't forwarded to the house when I saw this guy coming from the side of the house. To tell you the truth, he looked familiar. When I asked him if I could help him, he said he was looking for his cousin E-man. I told him that no one by that name lived here, so he drove off in a blue Toyota.

On my way to work we discussed going to court with the tenants and starting over with both homes. It was a fairly good conversation. We weren't bothered the least by the smoke in the air. We figured it was nothing out of the ordinary, just the factories overlooking Queens Bridge and the Fifty-ninth street area. I wished him luck on his job interview, and we kissed goodbye. I don't think we did that in a long time, kissed each other without anything behind it. To tell you the truth, I don't think we did much of anything in a long time. It was always something going on, but now things are going to be different. I just know they are. I could feel it. As I walked inside of the group home, my staff was asking me if I heard the news that a plane crashed. Truthfully speaking, we weren't even listening to the radio in the car. Before you knew it, another plane had crashed, and the announcer had then announced on the television that we were under terrorist attack. We saw pictures on television showing the crash into the twin towers. At point we tried to reach two of the girls from the group home through their cell phones. One was on her way to work in the city, and the other was on her way to school. We had one teen mother and three infants in the house, and they were safe.

I had to make a decision. I had two staff in the house. One staff had just completed the overnight shift and lived in Far Rockaway, and the other staff was just coming into her shift. She lived in Brooklyn. I called him on his cell phone, and he said he was stuck in traffic. I just knew he was in the city, but he told me that he was still in Queens. He didn't know about the terrorist attack. He thought there was some kind of accident. I told him what was going, and he decided to turn the car around and pick up the kids. I called my supervisor and told her that I was sending the staff home and that I would stay with the mothers and babies. I also told her that two of our mothers were not home and that we could not get in touch with them, but we will keep on trying. I also told her that he went to pick up my children and that they would be coming here to stay with us until we could figure out what was going on, she said that would be fine as a matter of fact I would prefer for the staff to stay because it might not be safe for them to travel.

The staff from Far Rockaway left, but the staff from Brooklyn said she would stay and help. She stayed and helped me reach the other residents. They were already on their way back to the house. The babies were quiet, and the other resident was calm. We didn't know what else to do, so we made the best of things here in the house. My children arrived, and the residents arrived at the same time. Everyone was safe. We contacted the 4-12 staff and the overnight staff to tell them not to come in, but they said they were coming anyway. At this point the house was full of staff, residents, and my children. He was sitting on the sofa. I guess he felt a little uncomfortable with a house full of women, so he went outside to talk the male neighbors.

I gave all the staff emergency instructions and his cell phone number as well just in case they could not reach me. I also called my supervisor to tell her that all the residents were safe and the house was covered, so I went home. We got home, and the kids were happy that the lights were on. It was a relief that it wasn't as cold in the house as it was last night, but the house still had a chill. We started cleaning up, and he started the boiler. My neighbor knocked on our door and told us that some guy came to his house looking for his cousin, and he told him that he must have the wrong house. My neighbor thought he might have been looking for our house, so the man said he would return when he thought someone would be home. As he walked down the stairs, I asked my neighbor which way did that guy go, he said he drove around the corner in a blue Toyota.

We sat up kind of late with the kids talking to them about today. I wanted to know their thoughts and feelings. They seemed to be okay, but with kids, you never know. Now that I know everything is going to work out, we could focus on our family and the children's future. He asked the children about their bedroom now that we had enough space to give each child their own room. We were looking forward to spreading them out. We talked about what color they wanted their rooms to be—one said blue, one said pink, and one said yellow, one even said pink and yellow. I agreed with all, but I had to get back to the one who wanted pink and yellow. It was nice talking to our children. We got a chance to learn about what they do in school, what their favorite subject was, and what they wanted to be when they grew up. I guess they were having their own little meetings while all of the chaos was going on in the house because they all said the same thing when asked what they want to be when they grow up. They all said at the same time they wanted to grow old.

Epilogue

He was originally from Brooklyn and born and raised a Baptist, and I was born and raised in Queens and born a Catholic. I don't think we really got a chance to learn about one another. Things just happened, and somehow we fell together. I don't know if you would call that love, but what I do know is we have the opportunity to find out what it is. We went to church today as a family. It started out a pretty good morning, and things just started getting better and better as the day went by. We ate breakfast together for the first time in a long time. He showed the kids where he grew up in Brooklyn and the church he served as an altar boy and where he wanted his sons to serve as altar boys. We drove past the church where I made my first communion, and hopefully, where my girls will make theirs.

We took the kids to the bike shop as a surprise to buy them all new bikes. We even thought about getting bikes for ourselves, but I couldn't imagine putting this seat on that seat. We were having such a good time that we decided to eat out and maybe watch a movie, but the kids had to go home and change their clothes. On the way home, I got a call from the group home and was told that one of the girls were thinking about leaving the group home. She had got into an argument with her boyfriend over the phone and decided now that she was eighteen she could leave and live with him, and she was right. She could leave, but was she ready to leave?

We stopped by the group home so I could talk to her, and by the time I got there, she was all packed and ready to go. She said she knew what she was doing and that no one was going to stop her. She said she loved him and he loved her. Of course she wanted to go with him. He was an older man with a car, and he had his own place. I asked him if he would take the kids to get some ice cream while I talked to her. I asked her why was she crying. She said because she loved him. I told her if she loved him, then she wouldn't be crying.

I told her love is supposed to make you laugh, not make you cry. After all of that, she said she didn't know what to do. She said she really didn't want to go, but if she didn't, she would lose him.

We spoke for a little while, and I asked her if she didn't mind if I called him to speak with him. She dialed the number and we spoke. He agreed with most of what we were discussing. He also said that he wanted her to wait until she was twenty-one before he would marry her. After talking to him and then her again, she agreed to stay. I called the social worker who would meet with him and her on Wednesday. I told the staff that she could get a phone call from him this afternoon after her chores were complete and her baby was ready for bed. As I was leaving, the staff told me that someone came by the house in a blue Toyota looking for his cousin, but he realized he had the wrong house.

It started getting late, and the kids looked a little tired. I asked them if it would be okay to go to the movies next week before we pick up their bikes on Saturday. They had a long day, and they were half asleep, so we drove home. I needed to speak to him about this blue Toyota that seems to be showing up all of a sudden. We were heading down the block and just about turned into the driveway when we saw this blue car speeding out of the alleyway. It nearly hit the tree next to the house. As the car passed by, the driver looked at him and said, "Hey, cousin." I asked him when we got out of the car and headed up the steps to the front door if he knew him. He said no. I told him that his face was familiar, but I wasn't sure where I had seen him before. He carried Heaven into the house, and I had just thrown my keys into my pocketbook when Wise asked if they could ride their new bikes to the park on Saturday. That's when it clicked.

BLAQUE DIAMOND

Did you ever know you were my heroes?

Beauty You came through for me in so many ways during some of
the most important times in my life. You have showed
me what a role model is all about and how to play the role.

Thank you, big sis.

Coffee I wanted to be like you when I grew up, even after the time you
ditched me to go to Coney Island with your friends. I now know
why you wanted me to just be a kid.

Thanks so much.

Phar You make things happen. You are the true magic man in my life.
You came through when all else seemed to be failing. You make
things happen.

Thanks for always treating me like an adult

Self You believed in me even when you thought I was wrong. You
trusted me with your most treasured treasures, Iyleah and
Heaven.

Thank you for our girls.

Tango	You are my left and right arm. You walked me down the aisle, You cooked for me throughout my three pregnancies. You even sat on the stoop late at night and helped figure out how to get rich schemes. Sorry I had to back out from jumping in front of the speeding truck, but you have to admit that would have hurt.

Thank you, Tango.

Melo	You challenged my every move from raising your son to fixing up the house. You helped me realize that power is not something that is given to you, it's something you take

Thanks.

Quick	Believe it or not, you are one of the smartest men I know. God Bless You and believe in him because he is real.

Truly I mean it.

Mommy and Daddy. I finally had something to say. Thank you for my voice.

Thanks for the closure.

CPSIA information can be obtained at www.ICGtesting.com
Printed in the USA
LVOW07*1426020215

425345LV00002B/35/P